Have You Ever Had A Hunch?

Other books by Ellen Palestrant

Nosedive
Johannesburg One Hundred
Remembering Dolores (co-editor)
I Touched A Star In My Dream Last Night
Pretzel on Prozac: The Story of an Immigrant Dog
The World of Glimpse
If You Can Make It, Mr. Harris…So Can I
If You Can Make It, Mr. Harris…So Can I: Teacher's Guide & Workbook

Have You Ever Had a Hunch?

The Importance of Creative Thinking

Ellen Palestrant

epCreative Enterprises

Have You Ever Had a Hunch? The Importance of Creative Thinking

All rights reserved
©1994, 2005, 2014 Ellen Palestrant (text, cover painting, and illustrations)

Third edition

No part of this book may be reproduced or retransmitted in any form or by any means without the written permission of the publisher.

ISBN 978-0-9848852-1-3

Published by epCreative Enterprises

Cover and interior design: The Printed Page
Author photo: Eric Cosh

Categories: Creativity / Education / Psychology / Independent Thinking / Self-Help / Art / Creative Writing

Printed in The United States of America

*To black coffee, for allowing me the extra hours so
necessary to complete this work.
To Nossi, Laurence and David, for nourishing all
the hours of my life.*

*To the USA for being my
Creatopia.*

The Penguin critics vie with one another in affirming that Penguin art has from its origin been distinguished by a powerful and pleasing originality… But the Porpoises claim that their artists were undoubtedly the instructors and masters of the Penguins.

Penguin Island by Anatole France (1908). Translated by A.W. Evans.

Contents

Dedication v
Preface xi
Introduction 1
The Hunch 7
The Hunch Crunchers 17
    A Hurry-Up Culture 19
        We Are Saturated 21
        Our Children Are Saturated, Too 24
    Lack of Solitude: 29
        No Place To Be Alone 31
        No Ability To Be Alone 33
    Instructional Intrusion, Emotional Intrusion 37
        Drill and Kill 39
        A How-To-Feel Nation 43
        A How-To-Feel-Ill Nation 44
        Categorical Apartheid 46
        What *Do* You Do? 47
        Overspecialization 49
    Judgmental Intrusion 51
        Expectations 53
        Evaluation 55
        Criticism 56
    Repression: 67
        Group Thought 69
        The Silencers 71
    Inauthenticity 77
        A Mindless Existence 79
        An Otherself 79

        Reliance On Role Models 81
        Visible or Valuable? 82
        Resumed 84
        Networked 85
    Fear **87**
        Fear of Risk 89
        Fear of Failure 90
        Fear of Being Different 91
        Blinkered Thinking 93
        Negativity 95
        Dogmatism 97
        Solution-Bound 98
        Rule-Bound 100
        Role-Bound 101
    Dream Deprivation **105**
        Severance from Night Dreams 107
        Severance from Daydreams 109
        Severance from Self 110
        Severance from Childhood 111
    Prerequisites for Creativity **115**
        Stock-Taking 117
        A Concept Is Not Enough 118
        Purpose and Commitment 121
        Sacrifice 123
        Passion—Not Flashin' 124
        Joy 125
        Deadlines or Dead Lines? 127
        Empathy 128
        Connectivity 130
        Adaptability 131
        Collaborative Creativity 133
        Humor 140
        Decision 141
It's Time For Lunch **143**
Text Bibliography **151**
Quotation Bibliography **156**
Index **159**
Quotation Index **167**

Preface to the Third Edition

Why Create

Ever since I was a child, I have felt an anticipatory excitement before beginning something creative. Even today, my fingers still literally tingle before I start, and this sensation is usually accompanied by feelings of joy, expectation and optimism. It would be hard for me to be severed from the creative process.

So why have I always had this ongoing need to create, and in so many diverse yet interconnected areas? And why do I enjoy encouraging others to experience the satisfaction of creativity as well? Why do I love creating and why do I continually explore the subject?

Firstly, because creating is positive, exhilarating—and fun.

We create to know what lies buried within us, and to be delighted with what emerges.

We create to be replenished by the actual process of the doing.

We create because we are moved to do so, and because creating offers the adventure and challenge of finding answers from within and not only from external sources.

We create to open that mysterious source that springs from deep within us.

We create because a life devoid of creativity is often a life lived on the surface, mindlessly adhering to other people's agendas—an unexplored life.

We create over a lifetime, sometimes never letting go of an idea that has become an intrinsic part of us.

We create because we have the courage to do so. We know that it doesn't matter if we fail; at least we tried, and in fact, a so-called failure could well prove to be a lucky accident—something, perhaps, aesthetically pleasing, and an opportunity for new experimentation.

And even for those of us who are experienced creators, we constantly need to encourage and permit ourselves to create in our very own way, instead of imitating what others have done - or what we, ourselves, have done successfully in the past. We remain open to the new, and therefore do not copy, conveniently and habitually, our own act that has worked so dependably in the past, instead of upping our own ante. We never try to disregard that barely verbalized thought or feeling - that glimpse of possibility—that enters our minds unbidden. We know that there is the potential in the unexpected and therefore it is important to listen to our instincts or hunches and follow them. We give unexpected ideas a chance.

The act of creating continues to fascinate and satisfy me. For me, and for so many of us, creativity is a direct springboard to much that is positive in life. It is the catalyst to becoming energetic, vibrant, joyful, generous individuals and contributors to society. Music, the arts, film, and profound literature, transcend cynical propaganda and therefore unite, rather than divide people. They are bridges to human connections and individual and collaborative inventions. Those who create, have much to offer the world.

I have expanded and updated HAVE YOU EVER HAD A HUNCH? The Importance of Creative Thinking; it is now in its 3rd edition. There is nothing static about creativity and, therefore, both my curiosity and knowledge about the subject continue to expand. The subject of creativity, in its many shapes and forms, will always enthrall me.

So, whatever your age, just remember that by creating, you enrich your own life and also the lives of other. A life devoid of creativity is barren for both individuals and societies. Creativity makes you self-reliant. Creativity is your companion for life.

Introduction

As members of society, we are attached to strings—to certain behavioral agreements essential to reasonable group cooperation. If, however, our ability to follow our independent hunches confidently and courageously is impaired, and if our spontaneity is curtailed, these restrictions become *hunch crunchers*, inhibitors that strangle creativity.

If we hope to progress, therefore, we need to understand the many influences on our lives, embrace some, reject others, and then, despite these strings and because of them, confidently follow our hunches into a world of creativity. There will always be problems to face and strings attached to almost all we do, but we can still be creatively free. Instead of regarding these strings as reasons for not attempting new enterprises, we can be challenged to incorporate restrictions *creatively* into what we do, or transcend their boundaries.

Because our world is changing so rapidly, most of us will need to adjust periodically to new and often confusing circumstances. Our best way to plan for tomorrow is to prepare for tomorrow, and to be ready, we need to be adaptable. Few of us will have only one career throughout our lives. Our economic, political and social situations will alter. So not only is it important for us at present to have a deep knowledge of our field of work and enjoy the security of our family and social environments, but, should the necessity arise, we also need to be able to skillfully create and accommodate new work and social circumstances. We will probably have to recreate ourselves in varying degrees many times during the course of our lives. For us there will be many beginnings. Creativity is about beginning. It is also about completing what we begin.

Many people are more adept at creative thinking than they realize, but haven't had the opportunity to discover that capacity within themselves, nor sought the adventure (and challenge) of finding their answers from *within* instead of from external sources. Too many individuals simply haven't had the experience of creating independently or collaboratively, and creativity comes with *practice*. It also comes from self-direction, self-motivation, self-actualization, and from learning not to rely *only* on known sets of solutions.

In order to unleash their creativity, people need to understand the obstacles to their independent thinking. Their creative restrictions have come from a variety of inhibitors, accumulated and passively accepted over the years. These have stood in the way of their perception of the extent of their abilities, and have caused many to lack the confidence and courage to try new things, and bring them to fruition. Too often, individuals, quite wistfully, regard areas that intrigue them as being outside their domain, and therefore do not dare to attempt them.

This is not, however, a "how-to" book, but rather, a "what stands in your way" one. There are no methods I wish to impose, no recipes for instant success. I do not want my direction to stand in the way of you and your originality. Instead, I would like you to recognize what has historically impeded you and prevented you from following your own hunches. By identifying these hunch crunchers, you will be freed to value your own intuitions, find your own path to creativity, and hence your potential.

While reading this book, you might also enjoy the affirmation that many things in which you believe, many ideas that at times have set you apart from others, *are*, in fact, valid, even though you hadn't realized it before. What has *felt* right for you *is* right, and your hunches are indeed worthy of your attention.

The Hunch

> My own experience of inspiration...a dim cloud of an idea which I feel must be condensed into a shower of words.
>
> Stephen Spender,
> "The Making of a Poem"

Have you ever had a hunch, followed it and been proven right? Or wrong? Nearly right, perhaps? Have you ever had a hunch, not followed it, and subsequently wished you had?

A hunch is your response, your automatic reaction to a stimulus which has not been influenced by logic. It is often accompanied by a feeling of confidence. A hunch is intuition. It *feels* right even though it has not been preceded by reasoning and has yet to be verbalized. It is a glimpse of something whole that needs to be focused upon and explored before it is analyzed, dissected and defined. That hunch or glimpse of possibility needs to be trusted; it contains something of a truth within your grasp, something to which you are trying to give a permanency. Rejection, if necessary, can come later.

You need to give a future to those unexpected hunches, otherwise they might be lost forever. Those hunches are your points of departure. They might take you on journeys without clear destinations, without the dependable impositions of known routes, but those mysterious and intriguing destinations will be discovered. The unintended detours and accidents—or dead-ends—are marvelous opportunities to develop the sense—aesthetic, scientific, technological, commercial or philosophical—of where you want to go.

A hunch is thought to be right-brained, complete, yet it has to be developed, to be delivered from within to the exterior. It is subjective and primary, and is the seed, image or prethought that, if followed by your attention, often leads to discovery and creativity. The hunch, accompanied by a quick flash of recognition, a moment of clarity and an intuitive understanding of reality, is the *epiphany*. It is the perception of something commonplace in a new light. It's seeing, what Irish novelist James Joyce called, "its soul, its whatness," that "leaps to us from a vestment of its appearance." He called the short stories and sketches of his collection *Dubliners* epiphanies.

Alternatively, instead of feeling an instinctive attraction to that fleeting glimpse and an accompanying desire to explore the stimulus further, you might, instead, experience an instant recoil from it, or from a vision, an idea, thought or person. That automatic rejection is generally valid, and, therefore, informative in clarifying what feels right for you.

> The idea came to me without anything in my former thoughts seeming to pave the way for it....
>
> **Henri Poincare,**
> A*The Foundations of Science*@

Isaac Asimov, who had a doctorate in chemistry and who during his lifetime wrote more than two hundred books on subjects as disparate as biochemistry, physics, history and the Bible as well as science fiction stories and novels, referred to himself as an "explainaholic." One of the areas he examined (and explained) was that of original scientific ideas and their genesis. He suggested that naturalists Charles Darwin and Alfred Russell Wallace, who had each arrived independently at the theory of evolution, were intuitive because they both had "the gift of seeing the consequences 'in a flash'…of feeling what the end must be without consciously going through every step of reasoning." Innovation, he said, came from people with a "greater capacity for dredging the combinations out of the unconscious and becoming consciously aware of them."

A sensitivity to hunches is apparent in the creative process of many notable scientists and thinkers. "He would get this unstudied insight while the problem was still being read out," observed a high school teammate of Nobel Prize winner Richard Feynman, whose theory of quantum electrodynamics was confirmed to have greater accuracy than any other theory of nature. Feynman apparently arrived at mathematical answers almost intuitively. It came from a knowing from within—"intueri"—from a fleetingly illuminated feeling of knowing.

Physicist Albert Einstein also had the ability to get to the essence of things quickly and instinctively. When he was caught one day in a sudden downpour, he hastily removed his hat from his head and placed it under his coat, according to Banesh Hoffman in *My Friend, Albert Einstein*. Einstein explained he did this because his head but not his hat could withstand the moisture.

According to Silvano Arieti, New York Medical College Professor of Clinical Psychiatry and winner of the 1977 National Book Award in Science, even though intuition is "a kind of knowledge that is revealed without preparation or as an immediate method of obtaining knowledge," it does, in fact, arise from many prior stages of preparation, including primitive organizations of past experiences, memory traces and images.

Intuition, or the hunch, that elusive, exciting, transcendent feeling, defies definition as much as does its offspring, creativity, which is equally confusing, energetic, hazy and fascinating. Both occur outside the bounds of human cognition. It is hard to define a hunch or creativity precisely. By demarcating either into clearly defined areas, a disservice would be done to their mystery and ambiguity. If we define a hunch as one thing, we ignore all the other things it is, too.

Similarly, if we define creativity within non-elastic borders, we exercise conscious control and cease to explore the barely accessible realms it inhabits. Even though the language of definition is useful, it can also be reductive. It can remove the creativity of creativity.

Unfortunately, that hunch, that barely verbalized thought that enters our mind so unexpectedly, is habitually disregarded, and therefore often lost—forever. It disappears because of our preconception that something spontaneous cannot possibly be significant. We often fail to realize that anything so seemingly small as a hunch can be the catalyst to a created form, or a successful scientific or commercial idea, that it can be something communicable, something of value—a fresh perception or a captured reaction. We've been told too often that significance comes only from hard work, book learning, traditional sources and the approval of authority.

In whatever we do, be it in the area of communication with our family, friends or the public at large, be it in the aesthetic, scientific, social, political, economic realms of work, we need to be receptive to our hunches. If we are not, our thinking, even though derived from logic, will be incomplete and dead. It will be devoid of instinct. In his essay *Paradise Lost*, Vaclav Havel, writer and leader of Czechoslovakia during politically unstable times, addressed the importance of instincts and politics. "It means having a certain instinct for the time," he said, "the atmosphere of the time, the mood of the people, the nature of their worries, their frame of mind." It is important for leaders to have an instinctive understanding of and empathy for the people they represent—and the times in which they live—if they are to be positively influential. It is important for artists, too, to remove conscious control and allow fleeting images into their own awareness and be open to their development because real art arises from an internal necessity, from the essence of the artist, and not from a devoted adherence to the style of the day.

We need to listen to our instincts or hunches. We need to follow them because they excite us to enter new creative worlds. They direct us to embrace initially intimidating, but challenging projects. They give our lives the richness of experiences: of joy, frustration, sacrifice and satisfaction. Our hunches are easily transportable; we can take them anywhere. They demand no space other than what we have available in our heads. These hunches, which we all at times have, tell us we can achieve. They are the starting points of our creativity.

Creative people respect their intuitive stages and transform the vague into the aesthetic, the scientific or the commercial product. They translate their hunches into reality by removing conscious control and allowing images, instincts, feelings, into their own awarenesses. They acknowledge what's within and invite out those images and feelings that inhabit the interior worlds of their minds. Creative people are receptive to their hunches.

You too will be creative if you acknowledge and respect the unique material that dwells within you and allow it to take its own form. You need to pay attention to your feelings, to listen uncritically, to always be willing to take *your hunch to lunch.*

Dear Hunch,

You are spontaneously invited to lunch.

Venue: Anywhere

Time: Anytime

But

R.S.V.P. Don't Delay
          Indefinitely
          It Might Soon Be...
          Past Hunchtime!

Taking your hunch to lunch should be easy, but it's not. Obstacles stand in the way. These barriers judge, condemn, inhibit and drain you of an ability to listen freely to your hunch. They deny you access to an essential route to reaching your creative potential. They compete with your hunch and shout more loudly. These destructive, negative controls, which pounce on intuition, ideas, feelings, as soon as they surface and bury them in conformity and insignificance, are the *hunch crunchers*, and they rob people of their potential.

These hunch crunchers scream messages suiting their own agendas, and even if much of what they say has value, some recommendations are manipulative and prevent people from becoming self-actualizing. Humanistic psychologist Abraham Maslow developed a theory based on a hierarchy of motives. Even though he placed self-actualization at the top of his hierarchy, he saw the fragility of this motive because there were so many needs at lower levels that crunched people's potential. These crunchers function at inferior levels to your hunch, but they are powerful influences.

The road to reaching self-actualization, and therefore reaching your potential, is fraught with disturbances. Because of this, before you are ready to lunch with your hunch, you first need to identify the obstacles or crunchers in your life and free yourself of them. Norman Cousins, author, lecturer, and for forty years editor of *The Saturday Review*, observed, "Death is not

> It's about removing barriers, which is one of the few straight-forward things we can do to encourage creativity.
>
> *Nathan Myhrvold, Senior VP, Advanced Technologies,*

the greatest loss in life. The greatest loss is what dies inside us while we live."

Therefore, while you live, nurture and cultivate your potential. Otherwise it will die, and you will have failed it. The creative path is seldom easy. Remember, as Benjamin Franklin said two hundred years ago, there is "no gain without pain." Remember, too, that there is seldom instant achievement. Instead, it can take "twenty years to make an overnight success"—as comedian and writer Eddie Cantor said in a *New York Times* interview.

I hope you won't have to wait so long. I hope, too, that after reading this book and identifying the major obstacles to your creative thinking, you will be ready to take charge of your potential, feel secure with your own originality and be motivated to create and create and create, for the next ten or twenty years—for however many years it takes.

The Hunch Crunchers

A Hurry-Up Culture

Too Little Time, Too Many Choices

> There is more to life than increasing its speed.
>
> **Mahatma Gandhi, Hindu Nationalist Leader**

> We haven't the time to take our time.
>
> **Eugene Ionesco, "Exit the King"**

We Are Saturated

"In America," said Swiss psychiatrist Carl Jung, "you can be anything. In my country I have not as many opportunities given to me. Therefore I dig deeper and deeper in order to find my own life."

Today, not only in America, but in many industrialized countries in the world as well, people have become overstimulated and overwhelmed by all the choices available. We are being pounced upon by ever-increasing technological advances and alternatives—some impressive, but many developed only because of perceived gaps in the market—and dependable advertising strategies for confusing the public even further. Too many options stand in the way of deep examination. People rarely have a moment's peace to contemplate or explore the bewildering information and excessive details they are fed—ad nauseum. There simply is no time for personal analysis of the never-ending, informational input they are expected to absorb.

The public is being bombarded by information, disinformation, by newscasters, *my*-view-casters, gossip-mongers, political opportunists, "experts" and their "expertise." Some are profound; others thoughtless, offensive, and unsound. Blitzed by options, by consumerism, by noise, Americans now also endure fear. They are aware that the terror attacks they experienced at home and abroad, came from groups who are still focused on their destruction, people who would rather *hate than create*. Americans brace for more violence, for climatic and economic disaster—for the next malevolent onslaught. They are in overload.

Political "experts" sell their pre-packaged thinking, financial analysts, theirs. Into whose interpretation of political events or economic eventualities should we buy? What commodity will reflect well on us? Which new fashions will enhance us? What cereal displayed in the rows and rows of cereals in the ultra-super-megastore should we choose? Which of the latest technological applications is best? How long will it take for it to become outdated? How do you keep up with the ever-changing future? How much more time will we spend trying to make choices? Will there ever be enough time to explore our individual creative desires?

In an external environment with so much information and choices, one in which we have to shout to be heard, and in an internal one in which our anxieties repress our creativity, it is exceedingly difficult to pay attention to our own observations, inner needs and intuition. We are so connected to this ongoing stimuli, to so many confusing perspectives, that we are deprived of a very important ingredient of creativity: spending time with ourselves.

> The pace of events is moving so fast that unless we can find some way to keep our sights on tomorrow, we cannot expect to be in touch with today.
>
> Dean Rusk,
> U.S. Secretary State,
> 1961-1969

People who are removed from their own instincts about things become increasingly confused by the multiple perspectives they are continually offered on issues, on goods, on desirable behavior. They become incapable of defining for themselves their own view of the world or even of their own lives. They suffer a loss of authenticity and commitment. More and more they turn to those whom they perceive have "authority" on spiritual, emotional and financial decisions, and more and more competing "solutions" are sold to them.

There is little time for in-depth investigation of possibilities, or even for deep investment into relationships with others. In his book *The Saturated Self*, Kenneth J. Gergen, professor of Psychology at Swarthmore College, investigated the relentless siege from competing alternatives with which we are all continually bombarded, and the dilemmas of choice this creates. He observed that an open slate had emerged today "on which persons may inscribe, erase and rewrite their identities as the ever-shifting, ever-expanding and incoherent network of relationships invites or permits." For many people today, the social—and anti-social—networks have altered dramatically the meaning of genuine friendships, real achievements and values—and an understanding of who we intrinsically are and what we truly require in life as opposed to what we are told we should want to be and what we should acquire.

There are increasing demands on our time. Paperwork, the media, computers, the Internet, Email, social media, telephone calls, needy people, financial realities, family and social commitments tug at us, demanding attention. We have become so many things to so many people and have begun to function in a disconnected fashion. What has occurred, according to Gergen, is the "fractionalization of self."

Some of us might have the discipline to work, but others often do not have the discipline to let us do so. We have been forced to become intermittent pursuers of our areas of interest or passion. We are unable to become fully immersed in what we are doing, and therefore our ideas and original perceptions become lost in a frantic world of constant action. This in turn leads to our creative inaction. We are on French dramatist Jean Cocteau's express train "hurtling towards death." We need to get off the train, take time to listen to our selves and acknowledge our own needs.

Our Children Are Saturated, Too

It's Saturday morning: many children's television, electronic and online programs beckon concurrently. Which one should little Lisa watch? Not only is she drowning in a technologically-saturated world, but, simultaneously, she is being enticed by advertisers with whom a relationship exists that has bypassed the mediating role of the parent. What should she buy, or rather, for which product should she campaign? Toys? Candy? Clothing? What brand or logo will enhance her self-worth, give her a whole new identity, and make her instantly popular with her peers?

This unabashed child-advertiser relationship started as far back as 1955, when a toy company, Mattel, invested half a million dollars to become one of the sponsors for *The Mickey Mouse Club*, and advertised its products on television for an entire year. But that was minor compared to today's ubiquitous "cradle-to-grave-branding." According to James McNeal, author of *Kids as Consumers: A Handbook of Marketing to Children,* kids, up to the age of sixteen in 2010, influenced their families in terms of spending to the tune of $1.12 trillion. And the markets continue to grow. To many merchandisers, children are synonymous with huge profits because of their vulnerable minds, and their power to nag. They must therefore be educated to shop or persuade their parents to shop for them. According to Susan Linn, director of Campaign for a Commercial-Free Childhood, "Marketers are getting more devious," with the increasing use of smartphones and social media.

Many children today are excessively busy. Not only does education dominate a child's day and compartmentalize it with programs promising opportunity, but the rest of the time—even during the school week—is taken up with the ever-beckoning entertainment on television, with online games, the Internet, social media, solicited and unsolicited Email and text-messaging, and all the other pre-packaged, playtime possibilities. Why should a child build a kite, for example, and *endure* the lengthy process of planning, patterning, cutting and gluing, when kites are available ready-made? Why make your own bubble solution or try different instruments for altering bubble shapes, when bubble pipe sets are already available in the store?

Children, thus, have little time to play in a world of their own creation. There is little time for fantasy, little time for imaginative, unconfined and unprogrammed exploration, little time for daydreaming, little time to read fairy tales or create them—even though fairy tales could play a significant role in the life of a child. According to psychoanalyst Bruno Bettelheim, fairy tales are necessary in the emotional development of the child. They convey a message that gratification is not generally instant and that "a struggle against severe difficulties in life is unavoidable, is an intrinsic part of human existence—but that if one does not shy away, but steadfastly meets unexpected and often unjust hardships, one masters all obstacles and at the end emerges victorious." And this is just what creativity is about—"mastering

> I take this as the first manifestation of the 500-channel world, with too many choices, each pretending to be revolutionary, when they=re almost interchangeable.
>
> **Robert Goldberg,**
> **TV critic**

obstacles" and "struggling against severe difficulties"—until the idea or that hunch is brought to completion.

In the United States today, it is the age of the microwave child, many of whom have never kneaded dough, never watched a meal being cooked from scratch. The ingredients are not of importance; it's the finished product that counts. Children are being consumed by consumables. These consumables are ready-made, and therefore, children are distanced from the process that brought them into being, because their relationships with them are relatively passive. A goal is achieved without the creative process, without the stimulation and sacrifice of work. Instead, there exists a need for instant gratification. Results are expected to be quick and are reliant on specific products that must be purchased; yet, we know that creativity comes from what is inside the child or adult and a tool is simply an aid.

In many countries, but in the United States, particularly, an industry revolves around programming the child, starting from pre-birth, and extending through babyhood and childhood. There are mothers who frantically flash cards in front of their six-month-old children because they have bought a program said to teach their babies to read. They have been told that such a goal is desirable. Accelerated learning franchises throughout the world are instilling numeracy, grammar, and pre-reading skills in children as young as two years old. The number of these centers is increasing as is the quantity of ambitious parents fearful that their babies will be left behind. Child-development specialists question the value of introducing formal educational programs to such young children.

Programmed children become programmed adults, believing that the purchase of instant knowledge in bite-size courses equals experience and the conquest of difficult tasks, when really they are merely fast-food substitutes, with little enduring nutrients. "I am doing a program on Ancient Greece" or "I am doing a program on world history," "on French literature," "on Chinese cookery" are simply what they are said to be—programs—outlines, pieces, lists, valuable titillations of giant areas of study, not to be confused with the years of sacrifice and commitment that a quest for deep knowledge and uncompromising creativity require. Sadly, in this very busy life of both child and adult, more choice means much less time, less substance, less depth and less originality.

If there was less choice of commercial, adult-inspired, child-directed entertainment, there would be more time for children to focus on and explore their own creativity.

Children need more time to be simply children and adults need more time to remember their childhood and how they once played.

If we are to cope successfully in a world of relentless choices, we have to know who we are and what we really need. That means we need to reclaim our time, wherever we can, and spend more of it creatively—spend that valuable time with ourselves, being ourselves, learning about ourselves and what we are able to do—by ourselves.

Lack of Solitude:

No Place, No Space, No Aloneness

> Solitude is blankness that makes accidents happen.
>
> *Robert Penn Warren, American poet and novelist*

No Place To Be Alone

There might be a place inside your head where ideas dwell, but having nowhere to bring these to fruition is a cruncher. Most creative people need a space, however small, to be their own and to use in their own way. Many people don't have this because of persistent realities such as financial restrictions that often mean too many people share the same space.

A home might have many inhabitants, each with their own needs. It becomes difficult for people in such situations to find a corner in which to be alone. Even if they find the physical space, the sounds of others continually break their solitude. Sometimes the physical space is owned by others and therefore under someone else's control. Sometimes, even their emotional space is invaded. In an environment that is hostile or excessively regulated, it is difficult to be creative.

The space in which we create, needs to be what Silvano Arieti calls "creativogenic." Some people need sunshine. Warmth and brightness enhance their creativity. Others prefer cool weather. A person can waste creative energy, however, searching for that perfect climate, that perfect place or that perfect solitude. Compromise is necessary. In terms of space, something very modest might do, simply a corner of a table in a kitchen or a worktop in a shed. Earplugs might help. Whatever you choose, or whatever you have to settle for, you can only hope that it will complement you and allow for the aloneness you require.

Not having an ideal place to work did not deter Elliot and Ruth Handler from going into production. Their garage in which they began making doll furniture in 1945 was the original site of Mattel, which by 1968 was ranked as a Fortune 500 company. In 1959, Ruth Handler invented the world's best known doll, Barbie. Wham-O, the company that made Frisbees and Hula Hoops, also started in a garage.

> When I am, as it were, completely myself, entirely alone...my ideas flow best and most abundantly.
>
> **Wolfgang Amadeus Mozart, Austrian Composer**

Gary Dahl initially did not have his own office space when he developed the Pet Rock craze. In fact, the environment which stimulated the idea was a rowdy one. It was 1975 and Dahl, who had a background in advertising, was in a bar in Los Gatos, California, when he spontaneously responded to a question about whether he had a pet with "Oh hell, yeah, I got a pet rock, man." Dahl then took the yet-to-be-focused-upon hunch that had accompanied this statement, seriously. Something as unlikely as a rock for a pet (of sorts) had commercial potential. By the spring of 1976, he had sold over a million of these uncuddly creatures.

Some people, though, insist that a room must have the right *feel* if their creativity is to be unleashed. Writer Margaret Atwood wrote that she knows someone "who feels he has to change locale for every new novel he begins. He believes that each place—each room or writing space— contains only a finite amount of energy, and that the act of writing sucks it out of the air like a vacuum cleaner, onto his pages."

The perfect environment is important to many writers. Annie Dillard wants "a room with no view so that imagination can meet memory in the dark." Raymond Carver would write in his upstairs study. "For many years," he said, "I worked at the kitchen table, or in a library carrel, or else out of my car. This room of my own is luxury and a necessity now." Vladimir Nabokov was contented with "a first-rate college library with a comfortable campus around it." Margaret Walker sometimes found the bathroom to be "the only quiet and private place" where she could write. "That was the only room where the door could be locked and no one would intrude," she said. E.B. White said that "a writer who waits for ideal conditions under which to work will die without putting a word on paper."

More important than finding that ideal space is finding what is inside your head, understanding your emotions and following your hunches. More important than the ideal space is spending time alone with yourself.

No Ability To Be Alone

There are people who have a fear of solitude, of being alone with themselves, of questioning, attending to and assuming responsibility for their inner motivations. Aloneness allows thinking. Some people do not like to think. Many prefer to block out any possibility of focused thought by listening endlessly to television or by habitually wearing their iPods. They choose to be mentally inactive and uncritically accepting of what is presented. Yet mental and emotional interactivity are prerequisites for creativity.

Some people require more external stimulation than others as a source for their creativity. They need the energy of the sights and sounds of the outside world to trigger their imaginations. Then, generally, they need quiet to form something with the emotions they have now activated.

For most people, however, solitude (an increasingly difficult state to achieve) is a requirement if they are to commune with themselves—seriously. Solitude is essential for individuals who wish to venture into the mysterious areas of their minds and discover what they really feel and what they are actually attempting to form or say. Writing, for example, is a solitary profession. Writers spend hours alone, months alone, years alone, completing their works. For them there is little time for normal social interaction, even though they might enjoy the company of others.

> Truly creative people usually are loners working in their own way at their own pace on their own subjects.
>
> **Robert C. Schank, Director Northwestern U. Institute for the Learning Sciences**

> Loneliness is your companion for life. If you don't want to be lonely, you get into TV.
>
> **William Styron, American novelist**

"I'm a sociable person who likes being with people," said Czechoslovakian leader and writer Vaclav Havel. He was commenting on the dichotomy in his need to be sociable on the one hand, and alone on the other. At the same time, he said, "I'm happiest when alone, and consequently my life is a constant escape into solitude and quiet introspection."

"Being alone is one of the most difficult things to learn," observed writer Tom Robbins. "You can't succeed if you can't spend time by yourself."

Aloneness is an important facilitator of creativity. Many images, whether clear or fleeting, occur spontaneously, and are hampered by external stimuli and are subsequently lost. Aloneness allows us a relationship with our intuition and the opportunity of giving it undivided attention. It implies a separation from others, but, as opposed to loneliness, need not be accompanied by unhappiness or desolation. For creative people, alonetime is generally welcome.

Instructional Intrusion, Emotional Intrusion

Thinkers by Number

> Not I, not any one else can travel that road for you. You must travel it yourself.
>
> **Walt Whitman,** "Song of Myself"

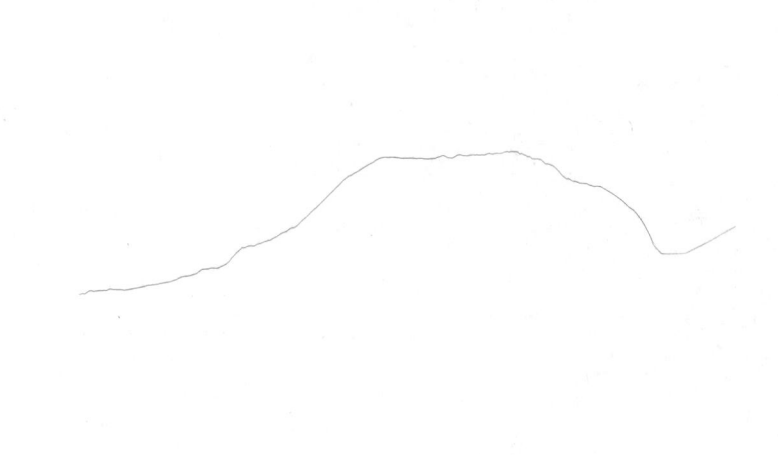

Drill and Kill

The role of education in any country is undeniably important, but when its role becomes one of intrusive instruction for almost every identifiable level of human action and interaction, it will lead to the emergence of largely robotic, predictable and exceedingly boring thinkers. What a nation will then have is an oversupply of the under-educated, for truly educated people have incorporated the uniqueness of their own vision into their thinking. They do not simply regurgitate the ideas of others. They do not become indelibly influenced by emotive instruction, numbed into non-thinking and distanced from individual responsibility. They do not become *Thinkers by Number*.

> I have never quite recovered from the psychological impact of a school report I received which I would not have believed possible had my mother not shown it to me. It read: "This boy shows great originality, which must be curbed at all costs."
>
> **Peter Ustinov,**
> **British writer & actor**

The prescriptive onslaught starts in childhood. Seventeenth century English philosopher John Locke believed children were born with minds that were *tabula rasa*, empty slates. Facts rather than the meaning behind them, answers rather than questions, have historically been the approach in education. Surprisingly, there are many teachers today who still believe that children need to be forcefed, and that students need to be encouraged to acquiesce passively. They do not realize that this crunches enquiry, curiosity and the venturing of individual opinions. "The school curriculum itself has always been the most stringent and persistent expression of adult-inspired censorship," observed communications professor Neil Postman in his book *The Disappearance of Childhood*.

Students are all too frequently faced with instructors who are bent on control, who assign curriculum hostile to enquiry. They will be taught that there is only one way, even though few truths are so solid that they must remain unchanged and unchallenged. In a 1954 *Peanuts* comic strip, Schroeder learned about an idea that could not be altered: the shape of the sun. He felt that a fluorescent light-like design for the sun would have been more practical than its present form, but, as Charlie Brown informed him, "It's too late to change it now."

It might be too late to change the sun, but it is not too late to change or modify many ideas. Educationalists need to be flexible in their approach to subjects if their teaching is to be effective. Adaptability is imperative.

There are critics who fear that flexibility in education will mean the neglect of the basic requirements—the three R's. In fact, these requirements would be better taught with active student involvement. Only bad or indifferent, non-creative teaching would adversely affect the basics. Drilling without understanding means facts are learned in isolation. Such knowledge is quickly forgotten. Knowledge, unaccompanied by self-discovery, will be poorly internalized and recalled.

Students need to be actively involved in their own education if they are to assimilate what they have learned, and this, fortunately, is something that educators have begun to realize. Education today is becoming more student-centered, integrated and dynamic. In many American institutions, students are no longer merely passive recipients of information; they are researchers and the explorers. The emphasis is changing. It is focusing more on process rather than on product; it is *active* as opposed to passive learning.

Exciting, new technology being used in many classrooms and homes today integrates interactive visual and auditory information, individuating learning and thus allowing for the differences in the way students learn. Students are being taught to learn independently, to be participative, to think critically, ask questions, to be doubters and expect evidence. They are being encouraged to challenge and not simply to embrace the assumptions of others. Students are no longer expected to accept a given solution without tangible proof.

There are countries where denying children (and adults) any opportunity of critical and explorative thinking is foremost in the political agenda. Instead of being *educated*, these children, from a very early age, are *indoctrinated* with hate-filled myths about the evil *other*. They are brain-washed into believing that their religion, their nationality, or their ethnicity is the only true or worthwhile one, and any one different should be punished, banished, or even, murdered. Independent thinking is fiercely forbidden.

These children (many of whom have been *drilled* to *kill*) have been robbed of their childhood, their intellectual and creative potential, and their future, Tragically, they grow up to be uncreative, unproductive, angry members of society who, in turn, perpetuate the philosophy of blame and hatred.

> Believing is a disposition. Thinking...is an activity, however sedentary. We could tire ourselves out thinking, if we put our minds to it, but believing takes no toll.
>
> W.V. Quine, *AQuiddities@*

It is important that children are not regarded simply as matterless and in need of being filled with what matters—to the educators or political leaders, rather than to the child. The starting point in teaching should always be the students and their needs. Education should not impose but should instead complement and stimulate students to seek answers. Neil Postman's often quoted remark emphasizes the stifling effect education can have on the curiosity of a child: "Children enter school as question marks," he observed, "and leave as periods."

Periods will beget periods unless children are encouraged to question, to be creative and original, to value their ideas rather than only the ideas they have been told are acceptable. It is of vital importance in a twenty-first century world, where cynical leaders use millions of *non*-individuals with no independent thinking skills as cannon-fodder, to encourage *all* children to become independent and creative thinkers. Educational curricula imposed on children are indicative of the adults they will become. Children, as well as adults, should be stimulated to pursue their perceptions, aspirations, and areas of interest, freely.

A How-To-Feel Nation

Instruction is big business. Not only do many educational institutions prosper from supplying information, but so do the producers of books, manuals, DVDs, audios and software. With efficiency, they provide valuable directives and educate numerous people on how to conduct a wide range of enterprises. Business techniques are learned from these products, and so, too, are construction skills, gardening, traveling, dating, loving, slimming, and countless other activities. "How-to" instruction helps individuals prepare for the job market, for motherhood, fatherhood, aunthood, new consciousness, new alternatives—many alternatives. Instructional communication, of all sorts, does a commendable job of catering to the needs of a wide range of people.

The availability of information in the United States is impressive, and so, also, is the efficiency and ingenuity with which it is delivered, as is the general consideration given to consumers, be it at educational institutions, at museum and art exhibitions, or trade shows. Knowledge is imparted generously.

Present sometimes in the dissemination of information, however, is a prescriptive approach. This does a disservice to an audience, especially when the information is strictly recipe-like in its delivery, when the instruction dictates *all* the ingredients, and the instructor becomes the controller, rather than a mediator simply pointing the way forward. Such instruction omits the differences in the experiences and impulses of individuals and distances them from their own

> For the mass in America today, the most powerful medium of education and information has become a surrogate of Linus's blue blanket. A ghastly glass teat.
>
> **Harlan Ellison,**
> *"The Glass Teat"*

instincts. Instruction, said to empower the recipients in some way, can, in a greater way, empower the dispensers of the information, causing them to be perceived as the only authorities on a subject, and the sole deliverers from evil.

Dogmatically prescribed ideas limit. Information designed to provoke individual thought, on the other hand, will stimulate people to seek further answers for themselves. They will see things more deeply and not remain bound by the information they have been given. "I went to the bookstore today," said humorist Brian Kiley. "I asked the woman behind the counter where the self-help section was. She said, 'If I told you, that would defeat the whole purpose.'" A "how-to" of any sort should promote independence of thought and not become a crutch for passive use.

A How-To-Feel-Ill Nation

Words influence the way we think. Vocabulary affects the intricacy of people's thoughts and creativity. They spur ideas that can subtly, or even vastly, affect people's perceptions of the world, often positively, but sometimes, in dangerously negative ways. When words are used purposefully to serve the ambitions or beliefs of totalitarian leaders, they can have the "tyrannical hold" referred to—in a different context—by anthropologist Edward Sapir whose Sapir-Whorf Hypothesis was once acclaimed. Words can encourage democratic values, creative thought, and new insights. Unfamiliar art terminology, for example, *Figuratively, Painterly, Fauvism, Abstraction,* might make artists see their own work differently—and guide viewers with their perceptions.

Language influences our perceptions in many ways. Words have emotional implications and associations that result in shared connotations, which often differ from the original meaning of the word, that is, from its actual denotation. Through language, English speaking people (who are not especially emotional) have become remarkably interested in identifying various emotional experiences. The English language, in fact, has more than four hundred words for feelings.

In the United States, particularly, English has become increasingly medical. American historian and writer Christopher Lasch in *Haven in a Heartless World*, a book in which he exposed the deception of a therapeutic society, called this phenomenon a "mental hygiene movement." American society has now become the patient, he observed, and the medicalization of religion as well has "facilitated the rapprochement between religion and psychiatry."

Recovery jargon is so popular in the United States that it is present in virtually every American home. So much of what we do has been given therapeutic significance, including creativity—where the palliative aspects are often stressed more than originality. We all know someone who is co-dependent or in denial, dysfunctional or in some twelve-step program. Millions of Americans are in recovery groups.

> Snake oils and sundry schemes to relieve aches and pains, to achieve wealth and success, and to make other desirable changes have usually enjoyed a brisk business.
>
> **Bernie Zilbergeld,**
> A*The Shrinking of America*@

It is fashionable to be in recovery. Such language has so influenced a nation's way of thinking about life that the United States can be perceived to be a nation in recovery. Habitual self-involvement arrests the development of creativity and keeps individual thinking primarily narcissistic or in a state of victimization. "It's no longer a question of staying healthy," observed humorist Jackie Mason. "It's a question of finding a sickness you like."

Categorical Apartheid

Leaders, educators, the media, marketers, slot and slot a lot. They mainstream, genre and sub-genre, often arbitrarily. They make something small into something big—useful for marketing but artificial because of its disconnection from the wider picture. Taught to pigeonhole their thinking, they then have categorical apartheid, severed from the whole, separate and therefore inferior.

Leader and writer Vaclav Havel rejected "binding categories," citing his "traditional antipathy to overly fixed (and therefore semantically empty) categories, empty ideological phrases and incantations that petrify thought in a hermetic structure of static concepts—the more hermetic, the further they are from life."

> The art of Biography
> Is different from Geography,
> Geography is about maps,
> But Biography is about chaps.
>
> **Edmund Clerihew Bentley,**
> *Inventor of Clerihew verse.*

Although categories or labels can be useful in organizing products and placing them in understandable areas, they can also be creativity crunchers. They limit thoughts to fit particular categories, slots or genres; they impose barriers between subjects that would naturally connect. They prevent the birth of something new because it doesn't fit conveniently into an existing niche. Ideas and hunches, which cannot be easily compartmentalized, are rendered homeless, and real creativity—organic, free-flowing, unique—is prevented from being unleashed. Categories or labels, instead of being constants, should be regarded only as useful suggestions.

What Do You Do?

The United States is indeed a label-intensive society. People are expected to define themselves and pinpoint what they do. If they do not give themselves labels, they are often regarded as unworthy of having one, of not having, in fact, attained any success whatsoever.

Even if people choose, out of conviction or defiance, not to wear a label, they find themselves placed in categories anyway because of the prevailing label culture. They might then be called "enigmatic," "interesting," "mysterious" or simply "a nobody."

"This, Linus, is what is known as a 'Flannelgraph,'" said Lucy, in a *Peanuts* comic strip. Obviously aware of the power of labels, she confidently gave this name to a few pieces of flannel she had tacked to a board. Poor Linus didn't yet know that these pieces had come from *his* blanket.

"I wonder how she thinks of things like this?" said Linus, pondering over her ingenuity. "A Flannelgraph! Just imagine!"

A label can hinder, but it can also help. In Lucy's case, it gave her meager enterprise an importance. Without a label, all she had achieved was the tacking of a few scraps of *stolen* fabric onto a board. She knew the strength of the label.

A limiting label curtails growth, whereas a label with growing room, encourages it. If you do not have a label for yourself, it might be useful to invent one. Why not become an *excuseologist*, for example, someone who specializes in inventing excuses for others, or a *vegimator*, someone who animates vegetables?

Once selected, a label can be a catalyst for growth within a specific area. When people who have drifted along finally define what they do, many then do it. In time, individuals may outgrow their labels and be pleased to move on, although others might be reluctant to let them do so.

> A good name is like a precious ointment; it filleth all around about, and will not easily go away.
>
> Francis Bacon,
> English philosopher

There are many well-known people who changed the labels they had once worn at some point in their lives. Somerset Maugham was a doctor who became a writer. Michael Crichton and Frank Slaughter were doctors, too, before they became writers, whereas Zane Grey was first a dentist. Singer Julio Iglesias was once a lawyer and so were actor Rossano Brazzi and comedian and writer John Cleese.

It is important to remember that a language of labels, though useful in the identification and development of concepts, can also stand in the way of our discernment of exciting, ambiguous and yet-to-be defined areas. The heavy, self-conscious and sometimes academic language describing a painting, for example, often has little to do with the mysterious creative spirit of the artist, and, if artists intentionally choose to fit into current styles with appropriate labels because they feel they are supposed to, originality and integrity are lost. The meaning given to a work can be a mere affectation or, even, decidedly false. A need to label to make something seem more important, can interfere with artists' creativity and render them dishonest. It can also make them discard what they are unable to categorize and lose potentially valuable work.

Overspecialization

It makes sense to specialize and therefore become proficient in a particular area, because the quantity of information available today is often overwhelming. A busy individual has a limited amount of research time. Overspecialization, on the other hand, can have a deleterious effect on a person's thinking. If areas of work are isolated and pigeonholed, they will lack connectivity. This can make an individual narrow and dull. It can also be a disservice to society because diverse subjects and professions nourish each other, and naturally overlap.

When people allow themselves only one designation, they cease to try other things. Ideas that do not pertain to their specialization are banished rather than integrated. There are ophthalmologists today who deal only with retinal disorders, orthopedic surgeons who only work on hands, and dentists who do root canals *all* day.

Many individuals abandon their areas of ability and even their deep interests because they do not appear pertinent to their work. Their daily lives become more and more constricted, and increasingly, their need for specialization leads them to less connectivity. Yet connectivity and freedom from boundaries are important elements of creativity.

> Specialist: a man who knows more and more about less and less.
>
> Dr. William J. Mayo,
> Co-founder of the Mayo Clinic

Judgmental Intrusion

The Pressures of Scrutiny

> Most of the advice we receive from others...is evidence of their affection for themselves.
>
> **Josh Billings**
> (Henry Wheeler Shaw),
> American writer

> The first man who objected to the general nakedness, and advised his fellows to put on clothes was the first critic.
>
> **E.L. Godkin,**
> "Problems of Modern Democracy"

Expectations

We all experience pressures from the expectations of others, whether in our relationships, at school, or in the workplace. As a result, we are often rendered self-conscious, nervous, anxious, defiant, even defeated. At other times, expectations have a positive effect on us by forcing us to go beyond what we perceive as our limits and achieve in a way we never previously thought possible.

Expectations are often hunch crunchers, however, and sadly, they lurk even within the most well-meaning of families. Early on, these crunchers sever children from their creativity, from something that came naturally to them and that had been so integral a part of their lives.

Expectations might sometimes encourage progress in children, but if they relate more to the needs of those in control than the needs of the children, they can be destructive. When children are expected to live up to artificial requirements divorced from their own aspirations, what often happens, in fact, is that they live down to them.

Expectations can be limiting and force children to assume personalities that are not really their own. Had their strengths and needs been recognized and respected, these children might have pursued their real interests passionately. Instead, they often spend

> Give me a child and I'll shape him into anything.
>
> **B.F. Skinner, American behaviorist**

the rest of their lives pursuing goals they have been told are worthwhile. Sometimes these children become aimless and stop pursuing anything at all. They have become disconnected from any internal drive.

Many children experience emotional stress because of ambitious parents or the scrutiny of an expectant public. As adults, they often become largely dysfunctional. For example, we have seen this with the British royal family. The children of Queen Elizabeth II, who were expected to perform in a way commensurate with their royal station, finally could not, and did not. We've seen this dysfunction with child movie stars and the children of the famous, who grew up under the ever-watchful (and critical) eye of the public. A genre of *Mommie Dearest* literature has emerged from this, which includes exposés by the children of Joan Crawford, the Reagans, and Marlene Dietrich.

"If the latter half of the twentieth century has taught us anything," observed author Robert Plunket in a *New York Times* book review, "it is that movie stars and first ladies should be real nice to their kids and document it."

> Creative minds always have been known to survive any kind of bad training.
>
> **Anna Freud, pioneer of child psychoanalysis**

The motivation for writing such exposes might be catharsis, or, simply, opportunism. With so available a target audience, who needs to be able to write? Whatever the reason, in one way or another, these children were hindered by family and public expectations.

Evaluation

Very often, the confidence of children (and hence adults) are crunched early on by standardized tests in the belief that all children are standard. I.Q tests are frequently regarded as the *only* measure of assessing ability. Although they are useful in predicting a student's ability to manage certain subjects at school, they poorly predict creativity.

Writer and biochemist Isaac Asimov saw a definite correlation between creativity and intelligence. He contended that the way people combine details is indicative of their intelligence. "The creative person must be able to combine 'bits' with facility," he observed, "and recognize the combinations he has formed; i.e., he must be intelligent...and recognize...some combinations are important and some are trivial."

There are other ways of testing ability. Professor of psychology and author Michael Wallach, for example, developed tests to predict creativity by measuring divergent production. He looked for ideational fluency, the ability to develop many ideas appropriate to a particular task.

Howard Gardner, educator, psychologist and recipient of the MacArthur Foundation Fellowship (the so-called genius award), feels that universally used I.Q. tests results in simply "short answers to short tests." He is convinced that there are better ways of understanding intelligence and assessing children's ability. In his book *Frames of Mind*, he identified at least seven types of primary intelligences:

> Do not worry about your difficulties in mathematics; I can assure you that mine are still greater.
>
> **Albert Einstein,**
> **Nobel Laureate**
> *in Physics to a student*

- ▼ Linguistic
- ▼ Musical
- ▼ Logical-mathematical
- ▼ Spatial
- ▼ Bodily-kinesthetic
- ▼ Intrapersonal, and
- ▼ Interpersonal.

According to Gardner, a person need not only possess one intelligence, but a blend, because "A blend of intelligences in an intact individual makes possible the solving of problems and the creation of products of significance."

Education, sadly, instead of being about the discovery of intelligences, talents or potentials, is often problem-based. In other words, if a child has a problem, that area is given attention at the expense of other areas. Therefore, strengths are ignored because they are not problems. Yet people will be most creative in their area of strength—that is where their potential lies. Hans Christian Anderson, a Danish writer of the nineteenth century famous for his fairy tales, bemoaned in his diaries:

> Unlucky me! Did miserably in Latin. You won't be advanced into the fourth form...Farewell to all my hopes and dreams...Why did the principal have to examine me in precisely what I have trouble with?

Criticism

How do you crunch a child? How do you crunch anybody? It is, actually, far too easy to demoralize a person. Most people have felt humiliated at some point in their lives, a consequence of the actions of those who need to aggrandize themselves at the expense of others. Fortunately, most people are resilient and are able to withstand any long-term ill effects.

Undermining someone's confidence can be achieved by dismissing an individual's ideas or contribution as being unworthy of attention, of being irrelevant, of having no basis whatsoever. By effectively exercising the pretentious art of dismissive arguing, one person can make another feel, simply, dismissed. When people's thoughts are continually disregarded, they soon see their ideas, and themselves, as worthless, whereas if they are listened to attentively and respectfully, they feel encouraged to pursue their thoughts and share them with others.

Creativity is both internal and external. Although its source is personal, the product is often public. The created product—the result of a creative process—elicits an aesthetic, critical and emotional appreciation in both the creator and the audience. It is an integration of the subconscious and conscious for both the producer and receiver at varying paces over a period of time.

Creative people face criticism of often their most valuable of possessions, their creative product. This renders them emotionally vulnerable to public opinion, and in extreme cases, even physically vulnerable, as we have seen with Salmon Rushdie, the author of *The Satanic Verses* whose life was threatened because of his creative product, his novel. The creative person originates something new, and therefore something that can be threatening.

Just because something is not accepted during its day doesn't make it potentially good or great. Sometimes, however, it is. Some critics are able to keep abreast of the times; others are disturbed by the unfamiliar and are unable to accept it. When first heard, the music of Stravinsky and Prokofiev were described as "aberrations." Having to listen to the music of Liszt and Strauss was said to be "agony." Tchaikovsky's music contained "savagery;" Wagner's, both "satanic fury" and "licentious discord" and Beethoven's was "repugnant" and "repulsive."

Anger at the new has frequently invoked furious invective: Chopin's music was nothing more than "ranting hyperbole;" it was "scrambling" and "perverse." Furthermore, he was a "nonentity." Beethoven was "obstreperous," while Ravel was not only "obstreperous" but also a "back-alley cat." Beethoven's music contained "odious meowing", Stravinsky's the "mooing of a young cow" and Bartok's the "mass snoring of a naval dormitory."

> The tough thing about success is that you've got to keep on being a success.
> **Irving Berlin, Russian-born American composer**

> If you want to please only the critics, don=t play too loud, too soft, too fast, too slow.
> **Arturo Toscanini, Italian composer**

For hundreds of years, criticism has played a major role in the arts, and critics have focused on different elements of the work, sometimes on the creator, other times on the creation itself, on its relation to and imitation of the universe and its effect on an audience. Employing different types of criticism to support their points of view, critics pass judgment on the value, quality, nature and purpose of a work. They generally value what they review according to established standards.

In the Middle Ages, criticism was based on the beliefs of ecclesiastical theologians who regarded literature, for example, as the servant of theology and philosophy. Something original was to be summarily distrusted. In the second half of the nineteenth century, however, literary criticism was viewed by poet-critic Matthew Arnold as an opportunity to "know the best that is known and thought in the world and...to create a current of true and fresh ideas."

Creative people often need the reviewer to establish their credibility. Generally, they want to be reviewed. Arguably, a bad review is better than no review, for it puts the creator in the public eye. It is risky to allow a creation out into the public domain; it is fearful not to. It is difficult, however, for creative people to achieve an immunity to criticism. What is being discussed is, after all, extensions of themselves.

The impulses of the critics vary:

They have been creatively moved to write incisive, informative, enlightening, amusing, witty, perceptive, sensitive, discerning, thoughtful, admiring, encouraging, deferential, complimentary, salutatory reviews

or

They have been creatively moved to write incisive, informative, enlightening, amusing, witty, perceptive, sensitive, discerning, thoughtful, unfavorable, uncomplimentary, cynical, reproachful, derogatory, censorious, hard-hitting reviews

or

They are incapable of being creatively moved.

The responses of those who have been criticized vary, too:

> Some creative flights are temporarily or permanently encouraged: others' creativity hovers directionless for long periods of time, unable to find the right way. Some people are thwarted or grounded forever—hurting. Others take stock and move forward more cautiously or more determinedly. A few continue to fly freely, accepting encouragement or reprimand as simply another lesson in creativity. They fly upward in pursuit of their hunches.

To withstand the negative effects of criticism, creative people need a strong sense of their own purpose, a confidence in their conception and an established sense of self.

That means they can listen to the critics and learn, but must always stay on course...

Judgmental Intrusion 61

How trite and feeble and conventional the tunes are; so derivative, so stale, so inexpressive!
Lawrence Gilman on Gershwin's ARhapsody in Blue.@

Lolita, light of my life, fire of my loins. My sin, my soul.
Vladimir Nabokov, ALolita@

Hands off my score! That=s my advice to you, Sir, or to hell with you!
Richard Wagner, in a letter to a teacher

I got rhythm, I got music....Who could ask for anything more?
George Gershwin, AGirl Crazy@

AAn American in Paris@ is nauseous claptrap, so dull, patchy, thin, vulgar, long-winded and inane.
H.F. Peyser on

Is Wagner a human being at all? Is he not rather a disease? ... He has made music sick.
Friedrich Nietzsche, ADer Fall Wagner@

Any bookseller should be very sure that he knows in advance that he is selling very literate pornography.
AKirkus Reviews,@ (1958) on Nabokov's

For critics I care the five hundredth part of the tythe of a half-farthing.
Charles Lamb, English essayist & humorist

Picasso enjoys making repulsive works out of beautiful subjects.
Raymond Mortimer, "Try anything Once"

I paint objects as I think them, not as I see them.
Pablo Picasso, Spanish artist

Charles Lamb I sincerely believe to be in some considerable degree insane.
Thomas Carlyle, Scottish essayist

Tell me, how did you love my picture?
Samuel Goldwyn, MGM movie mogul

The film suffers under its own weight and becomes tedious and heavy.
A*Rating the Movies,*@ on MGM=s A*The Good Earth*@

Judgmental Intrusion 63

Winston would go up to his Creator and say that he would very much like to meet His Son, about whom he had heard a great deal....
David Lloyd George, A*Diary*@

Attila the Hen
Clement Freud on Margaret Thatcher

In politics, if you want anything said, ask a man; if you want anything done, ask a woman.
Margaret Thatcher, British Prime Minister 1979-1990

She is trying to wear the trousers of Winston Churchill.
Leonid Breshnev on Margaret Thatcher

She is the best man in England.
Ronald Reagan on Margaret Thatcher

We are all worms, but I do believe I am a glow worm.
Winston Churchill, British statesman

If you must deal in criticism, confine your practice to self-criticism
A*The Little Red Book of Alcoholics Anonymous*@

64 Have You Ever Had a Hunch?

. Beethoven's one hundred and thirty-fifth work...gives evidence of an unbalanced mind.
AAmerican Art Journal, @1866

Advise your reviewers to be more circumspect and intelligent.... Your reviewers outcry against me was at first very mortifying.
Ludvig van Beethoven, in a letter to Breitkopf & Hartel

As a writer he has mastered everything except language...as an artist he is everything except articulate.
Oscar Wilde, on George Meredith

No passion in the world is equal to the passion to alter someone else's draft.
H.G. Wells, British novelist & historian

What a tiresome affected sod.
Noel Coward, on Oscar Wilde

God tells me how he want his music played—and you get in His way.
Arturo Toscanini Italian conductor

The critic leaves at curtain fall
To find, in starting to review it,
He scarcely saw the play at all
For watching his reaction to it.
E.B. White, American author & humorist

Judgmental Intrusion 65

To escape criticism—do nothing, say nothing, be nothing.
Elbert Hubbard, American author & publisher

I like only destructive critics, because they force me to...readjust my ideas.
Peter Ustinov, British writer and actor

Can't a critic give his opinion of an omelette without being asked to lay an egg?
Clayton Rawson, *No Coffin for the Corpse*

The temptation is tremendous to say that you like what you think you ought to like and don't like what you think you oughtn't to like.
Arnold Bennett, British playright & journalist

In the arts, the critic is the only independent source of information. The rest is advertising.
Pauline Kael, film critic

Comedy is criticism.
Louis Kronenberger *The Thread of Laughter*

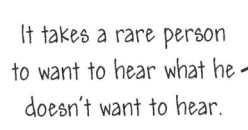

It takes a rare person to want to hear what he doesn't want to hear.
Dick Cavett, American talk show host

Repression
The Thought Patrols

> Human beings are perhaps never more frightening than when they are convinced beyond doubt that they are right.
>
> **Laurens van der Post,
> South African novelist
> & travel writer**

Group Thought

There are many kinds of groups: families, extended families, tribes, clans, villages. These and many other groups have, in varying degrees, sociopolitical, religious and economic bases. Groups can stimulate and nurture creativity because of a collective output of energy, love and caring. People need the affirmation of groups and the moral and structural guidelines they provide; the comfortable and comforting philosophies and religions, explanations of life and death, group identification and solidarity. Within groups are found love, friendships and shared interests.

Also within groups and between them are found fear, envy, competition and hate. The absolute truths of one culture, so unquestioningly accepted by a public, would not necessarily be the truth in another culture. Some groups or members of groups dominate, judge and decree, and often ruthlessly impose their *truths* on everybody they control. The more people they are able to control, the greater their power base. As German sociologist Max Weber observed, power is really about "the possibility of imposing one's will upon the behavior of other persons." Weber differentiated between "coercion," which encompasses physical force and fear, and "legitimate power," which has the consent of the people over whom control is exercised.

In most societies, however advanced, there is the presence in varying degrees of visibility and power of the thought patrols who are determined to nip ideas in the bud lest they become budding ideas, and, even worse, ideas that others might like, ideas that might steal minds or markets they already occupy or intend to capture. To such people, *same is the name of the game.*

These Thought Patrols disallow any type of thinking they haven't approved or prescribed. They fiercely and often violently promote *otherism*: the propensity to regard any one different, in any way (religious beliefs, national or ethnic affiliations, gender preferences) as an *other*, and therefore worthy of subordination, or even, elimination.

> There are good people and bad people in every community. No human race is superior; no religious faith is inferior. We all come from somewhere and we all wonder where we are going.
>
> Elie Wiesel,
> Nobel Laureate,

There are individuals, groups, and nations who identify themselves almost exclusively through the hatred of the other, and who, without this hatred, would have no identity at all. Ideologies of violence often accompany their paranoia. To achieve their political aims, they might effectively advocate doctrinaire solutions, banish people from groups, organize group action against them, deliver slogans in which they themselves might or might not believe, and rigidly enforce an adherence to these.

In a dialogue with Robin Skynner in *Families and How to Survive Them,* comic and writer John Cleese discussed the propensity of extremist groups for splitting up into more and more separate (and extreme) groups. Paranoia is always the dominant motive. In the British political scene, Cleese counted at least forty different groups in the "red corner" (the extreme left) and at least twenty "in the blue corner," (extreme right) complete with swastikas and various symbols from Nordic mythology. Cleese conceded he probably missed many because "they're all splitting up so fast, it's practically impossible to get the latest score."

Groups beget groups—more and more groups pulling in different political directions. Groups can beget people without critical thinking skills who become caught up in the various forms and intensities of popular hysteria. When this happens, they are incapable of making any independent judgments, but instead move with the mob. How individualistic the members of these groups are, how independently they think and how creative they are, depends on the intensity of group control.

> Liberated from an ideology I looked around at the world I was in and found myself besieged by ideologies. Rival ideas...laying claim to the world, including to myself.
>
> **Lionel Abrahams,**
> **South African writer**
> **& publisher**

Mob action and mob thinking often leads to violence. In a twenty-first century world, stockpiled with ammunition, biological and chemical weapons, nuclear arsenals, and maniacal thugs running rampant, mindlessness becomes ever more dangerous, and independent, responsible thinking ever more urgent. "At no other time in history," Woody Allen observed in *My Speech to the Graduates*, "has man been so afraid to cut into a veal chop for fear that it will explode."

The Silencers

Self-censorship is effective. It's voluntary and self-critical. Individuals as well as families and groups usually have a fairly casual agreement about what is right or wrong, what can or cannot be said.

When official, censorship will be embraced by the public—providing they are in agreement. In undemocratic societies, censorship needs to be extreme for those in power to remain in control. Such restrictions are effective, however, only because of coercion and the quantity of controlling measures continually introduced to reinforce the rules.

Totalitarianism disallows creativity, which it considers a threat. Ideas should not be more important than these people who govern with absolutes, often after having highjacked and reinterpreted the theories of others. Conflicting ideas are silenced.

Throughout the ages, intellectual terrorism and intense dogmatism have destroyed contrary opinion. They have crunched creativity. Examples of this are endless. In the eighteenth century, *Pensees Philosophiques*, the work of French philosopher Denis Diderot, was burned by the public hangman. Diderot was subsequently imprisoned for later writings that were too bold for his times. Manuscripts of Czechoslovakian Jewish writer Franz Kafka were confiscated in 1933 by the German Gestapo and destroyed. Books by South African writers, such as Alan Paton, Mbuyiseni

> You can kill a man but you can't kill an idea.
>
> Medgar Evers,
> Civil rights activist,
> assassinated in 1963

> Violence is the last refuge of the incompetent.
>
> Isaac Asimov,
> science writer
> & biochemist

Oswald Mtshali and 1992 Nobel Prize winner Nadine Gordimer, were banned during the years of apartheid. Russian writer Alexsandr Solzhenitsyn said that individuals were imprisoned in the earliest Soviet camps "not for purposes of correction, but to render them harmless, purely for quarantine."

Independent thinking continues to constitute a danger for both those in control and those they wish to control. Egyptian writer Naguib Mahfouz's life was threatened in Egypt in the name of righteousness after he'd won the 1988 Nobel Prize. There were death squads after writer Salmon Rushdie and after the bounty of millions offered for his capture. In retribution for his novel *The Satanic Verses*, a "fatwa" called not only for his death, but for those also who in some way facilitated the publication of his book despite being cognizant of its contents. There were attacks on bookstores, death threats to booksellers, publishers and supporters, and murder was committed. In an interview with writer John Banville, Rushdie said, "I have always insisted that what happened to me is only the best-known case among fairly widespread, coherent attempts to repress all progressive voices...always the arguments used...are the same: always it's insult, offense, blasphemy, heresy—the language of the inquisition."

A dichotomy emerges only too often in religion between spirituality and power, the latter injecting control, blackmail, fear and hatred. Many groups that were initially formed to fight oppression have been invaded by dogmatic, political ideologies that contain intolerant absolutes. When opposing political groups compete, there is a dangerous collision of ideologies. People have to be silenced. So does creativity. "Culture and fanaticism are forever irreconcilable," observed Elie Wiesel. "The fanatic is always against culture." So, too, is the fanatic always against creativity.

Diversity of thought is essential for creativity. Openness allows for abundance. A think-alike, look-alike world might have more ideological consensus, but it will lack cultural vitality. In 1991, in response to someone's suggestion of a world with a universal culture, eighty-two-year-old philosopher Isaiah Berlin declared that it would be "the death of culture. I am glad to be as old as I am," he said.

Because Americans do not live in a homogenous culture and do not share *all* assumptions, individual perceptions differ, often considerably. These differences, which sometimes lead to conflict, generally contribute positively to an exciting, cultural energy.

"What's American about America?" asked writer Ishmael Reed in a 1989 essay. It is, he then observed, a "blurring of cultural styles [that] occurs in everyday life in the United States to a greater extent than anyone can imagine," It is, he continued, what Yale professor Robert Thompson called "a cultural bouillabaisse." It is, according to writer and humorist Leo Rosten, green bagels on St. Patrick's Day, a product he pronounced "a feat of crosscultural fertilization." Diversity and cultural diffusion have been America's strength. So has creativity, a strength for all humankind and an endless resource for growth.

There has always been a need in humans to create. Palaeolithic artists drew and painted animals and men in caves thousands of years ago. There is a desire in people, too, to explore, to examine, to communicate, to explain and to eternalize. The art, knowledge and ideas of today are linked to thousands of years of innovation, to diverse cultures coming in contact with each other and making enriching and compatible contributions.

Individuals within diverse cultures benefit from the differences. They adapt, blend, and from the familiar and unfamiliar, build something new, integrating their personal feelings with external stimulation. American philosopher and social behaviorist George Herbert Mead spoke about the *me* within our personalities that represents the internalized values of society, and the I, that makes us unique. The *I*, as opposed to the *me*, cannot be penetrated by society. Both aspects of a personality are necessary. People who were not brought up in a rigid family or society usually have a stronger I within their personalities. This I needs to be preserved so that individuals will not acquiesce to the pressures of mob thinking.

A country, such as the United States, that represents a free society, allows for greater variety of conflicting, new, evolving ideas than do many other societies, and does not try to suppress them (even though individuals or groups within the country might). Silvano Arieti talks about a creativogenic society, a society that is conducive to creativity and offers possibilities if people have the potential. In other words, there are two important elements for creativity: a creativogenic society and a potentially creative person. Among the requirements of such a society, according to Arieti, are:

> Just to the left, and not very far away, were the Triple Demons of Compromise....Since they always settled their differences by doing what none of them really wanted, they rarely got anywhere at all—and neither did anyone they met.
>
> **Norton Juster,**
> A*The Phantom Tollbooth*@

▼ Fair and just laws

▼ Availability of and exposure to cultural (and certain physical) means, with free access for all to cultural media

- ▼ Exposure to and openness (on the part of the individual) to different and contrasting cultural stimuli
- ▼ Stress on *becoming* rather than *being*
- ▼ Tolerance for and interest in divergent views
- ▼ Interaction with stimulating people
- ▼ Incentives and awards that can make the creative person's life easier (and therefore more able to create).

Just as societies influence individuals, so do creative people influence their societies and their times. Sometimes their work is appreciated by only a limited audience and at other times by a much larger one because the political, economic, social and emotional climate of a country is now receptive to new ideas. Understanding society, its inflexibility, dynamism, inconsistencies or a combination of all three, is a prerequisite to comprehending our own creativity.

Inauthenticity
Just like Who?

If you see in any given situation only what everybody else can see, you can be said to be so much a representative of your culture that you are a victim of it.

**S.I. Hayakawa,
scholar & U.S. senator**

The wise man seeks everything in himself; the ignorant man tries to get everything from somebody else.

**Kung Fu,
Chinese martial art**

A Mindless Existence

In too many countries today, hatred mobilizes unquestioning masses (with patterned, repetitive ways of thinking) into nationalistic and religious fervor. This mindless adherence to the ominous philosophies and xenophobia of cynical and insane leaders, precedes ethnic cleansing, religious cleansing, and idea cleansing. Millions lose their lives. Hate leads to *destructivity* which is totally devoid of the positive in creativity.

> Where all think alike, no one thinks very much.
>
> **Walter Lippmann, American author**

A mindless or unexamined existence, without independent and creative thinking, is a perfect weapon in the hands of abusive leaders who promote group hatred, and who, in everyday life, crunch all creativity by forbidding questioning or freshness of vision. People who do not question become followers rather than thinkers. They become one-directioned and simplistic adherents of controlled *truths*. Divorced from themselves, they become *otherselves*.

An Otherself

People inexorably influenced by societal expectations are alienated from self and do not have established identities. These *otherselves* have traveled so far from themselves that they have little understanding of their own motivations, emotions, and impulses. Theirs is a life of ignorance, of inattention and imitation. The voices of others compete with their own, and eventually so condition their attitudes that they are barely capable of thinking independently. Instead of listening to themselves, they value only the voices of authority. They continually take direction from and imitate others. They expect their children to do the same.

Examples of good behavior are important and children learn from these. Sometimes, however, the emphasis is too strongly on the imitative. Children are constantly told that their originality and their way of viewing the world is not acceptable. There is a right way—*my* way, Mary's way, Jack's way, the teacher's way—certainly not *your* way. Children soon learn not to respect their *own* way. Family and peer pressure promotes imitation. It is imitation that gains them approval, even though, as Robin Skynner pointed out, "It's natural to be different, and healthy to disagree."

> Be what you is, not what you ain't, 'cause if you ain't what you is, you is what you ain't.
>
> Luther D. Price, philosopher

Sadly, what happens in childhood continues into adulthood. There are many adults who remain distanced from their real feelings or desires. They adhere blindly to the suggestions of others, neither questioning nor interpreting the motives of those whom they imitate. They ignore any hunch they might have because that hunch came from within, and they only respond to what comes from without. They are incapable of respecting their own originality. Such people become collectives, victims of homogeneous thought and actions, bent solely on maintaining a social consensus.

The self many people present is often far from real because it has been developed according to a commercial or cultural illusion—a politician, a sports personality, a movie star—all manufactured entities. Many people model their personalities, their interests, their dress, even their gestures upon what has been fed to them by their culture. In adopting another self, they become further and further removed from what they really are.

We have all come across people who are imitative. Conversing with them has been unsatisfying and largely a waste of time. This is because we have discovered we haven't been communicating with a person at all. Instead we've been talking to a structure.

If we are so removed from ourselves, so very derivative, how can we relate to our intuition and to our creative potential? How can we have the confidence to follow our hunches? How do we know that our opinions are really our own?

Reliance On Role Models

Positive role models are valuable and can provide hope, move people to emulation, and direct aspirations. Many of us are intrigued by the biographies of others with similar interests or goals. We learn from their work habits, their striving and philosophies. We feel less alone in our own struggles. Chairman of Microsoft William Gates "devours" biographies of high achievers in a variety of fields because he wishes to understand their thought processes.

It's a good idea for people to devour information about others, as long as they in turn are not devoured by their role models, and lose their identity in their attempt to be just like them. It is mindless to embrace others— who probably are largely illusions, anyway—so enthusiastically that all their ideas are unquestioningly adhered to. Not every idea of any one individual is good.

> One may be tempted to see the great man instead of the logic of the question.
>
> **Babylonian Talmud**

A role model or "star" can simply be an illusion. This is exemplified in Jerzy Kosinski's novel *Being There*, where Chance, a simple and uneducated gardener, becomes a media celebrity—by chance: "Chance became an image for millions of real people. They would never know how real he was, since his thinking could not be televised," wrote Kosinski.

The thinking of role models as diverse as Hillary Rodham Clinton, Queen Elizabeth, William Gates, Madonna, Mother Theresa, Michael Jordan indeed cannot be televised. The public image is a fragment of the individual. Yet, because of a fear of being themselves, so many people base their hopes for success on emulating that part-person whom they think they know. Not only do they blur the differences in the complex composition of their role models, but they also blur the differences between their own realities and those of the individuals they so closely try to approximate. No two lives can or should be entirely the same. Too often, people who have been fed unrealistic expectations become extremely disillusioned with the lack of parity.

Visible or Valuable?

People who base their actions and choices on their need to impress others are, in turn, also impressionable. In his book *The Culture of Narcissism,* Christopher Lasch discussed a current American society where "impressions overshadow achievements," where "what a man does matters less than the fact he has *made it,*" and where "those who win the attention of the public worry incessantly about losing it." That need for acclaim is not only a pressure, but a reduction, because it equates success with public endorsement and makes it reliant upon it.

All too often, being best is confused with whose image is best. People are constantly working at the image they present rather than the substance of their actions. This even extends to the way a public chooses political leaders by looking more at what is visible than at what is valuable.

"Image politics empties itself of authentic political substance," observed communications professor and writer Neil Postman, in his book *Amusing Ourselves To Death*. We look at our politicians on a television screen, he said, in the "same voracious way" as the fairy tale queen in *Snow White*. "Mirror, mirror on the wall, who is the fairest of us all?" we ask, and then, Postman said, we tend "to vote for those whose personality, family life and style, as imaged on the screen, give back a better answer than the Queen received." Not only are celebrities (including politicians) habitually seeking ways of being publicly visible, but so do many people translate even the most automatic or instinctive behavior into something worthy of praise. An expectation of public approval often accompanies the natural act of being a good mother, a supportive spouse, a caring child or a responsible citizen. A need to be visible makes many people into their own, live commercials, emptied of substance.

Doing something in order to be *visible*—visibly educated, visibly creative, visibly virtuous, visibly loving, visibly rich, visibly alternative, visibly conservative, visibly pious—instead of out of interest, passion and caring is a creativity cruncher. The motivation comes from self-interest rather than from an intrinsic need to help, share or create.

Creative people, on the other hand, have the capacity to look outside themselves and see their work and their world as bigger than themselves. They are not fearful of following their hunches or trying new things lest they become visible failures. They are not fearful of spontaneity and taking that creative leap. They have the courage to create.

Resuméd

People who need to be visible often try to acquire that admiration through the perceived success of their children. Ambitious parents and too many training regimes can take the joy away from exploration and instead create anxiety and resentment. They can create the *programmed child*. Such a child's need to explore is limited by schedules, programs, timetables, as well as an overabundance of stimuli awaiting attention. The programs selected for such children are generally chosen by the parents and often are more indicative of parental aspirations than of the children's. From early on, these children are encouraged to see life in terms of a resumé.

These children also do not have sufficient spare time in which to pursue a real or potential interest. They are continually interrupted by further scheduled activities, and therefore their absorption time in creative pursuits is incessantly obstructed. They often become shallow, self-conscious adults and convenient thinkers, because their areas of study or exploration were not selected passionately, but chosen primarily because they would look good on a resumé.

> If you wish in this world to advance,
> Your merits you're bound to enhance;
> You must stir it and stump it,
> And blow your own trumpet,
> Or trust me, you haven't a chance.
>
> **William Schwenck Gilbert**
> A*Ruddigore*@

Networked

Networking can be invaluable. It provides people with the opportunities for meeting others in their field or in related areas. It might even give them that lucky break—providing they have something to offer. An over reliance on connections, that is on the cultivation of others who *count*, however, rather than on actually *doing* the necessary work, can be a creativity cruncher. Individuals who constantly chase contacts become dependent on the perceived power of other people, rather than on being as good as they possibly can be at what they do.

> If you go up high, then use your own leg! Do not get yourself carried aloft; do not seat yourself on other people's backs and heads.
>
> **Friedrich Nietzsche,** *Thus Spake Zarathustra*

Fear

Imprisoned Visions

> Do not fear yourself,
> for that is your self.
>
> *Carl Jung,*
> *Swiss psychiatrist*

Fear of Risk

Fear is realistic. Imaginative, intelligent people fear danger, harm and evil. They naturally protect themselves and others— if they can—against gun-wielding maniacs, financial insecurity, loneliness, corruption, blackmail, illness and death.

It is the degree of fear and the related anxieties that can be debilitating and cause natural emotions to become creativity crunchers, limiting the capacity to follow hunches, try new areas, take risks, enjoy life and be productive.

There are times when you need to take risks and there are times when risk-taking is inappropriate. If the water is infested with sharks, don't swim, but if it is filled with ideas to be explored, take the plunge. Risk means venturing where others have not, or staying behind to give more attention when others seemingly move forward. Risk means looking at the known as if it were unknown, and examining the unknown until it is known. Risk can be a stimulant; fear, a cruncher.

> If the creator had a purpose in equipping us with a neck, he certainly meant for us to stick it out.
>
> *Arthur Koestler, Hungarian-born English author*

Fear of Failure

Fear of failure is often related to the critical voices in your head—your own, harsh voice of judgment or the voices of others who always find reasons to criticize—whatever you do. When facing the possibility of failure, it is a good idea to imagine the worst scenario, such as execution. Are you really going to be executed for your mistakes? The more mistakes people make over a lifetime, the more they have attempted and the more they have learned. Creative people make more mistakes than others because they try more things. As Albert Einstein said, "A person who never made a mistake never tried anything new." A mistake is simply an experiment from which to learn.

> Is there a person who has not made one error and half a mistake?
>
> *Chinese proverbial wisdom*

When you repeatedly make the same errors, it might be an indication that you need to put the task away for awhile and try a new approach or even do something quite different. You have to know instinctively when to continue and when to stop, when what you are doing has become an exercise in futility. Making mistakes might slow you down, but it won't prevent you from ultimately reaching your goal. Not learning from mistakes will.

It's sensible to remain realistic about your aspirations, but helpful to be optimistic. Why not imagine the best scenario—years of stimulation and joy from your work, self-actualization and success. To achieve this, you will need to commit to your dreams, challenge the rules and *risk*. Keep in mind that your potential will not fail you; you might fail it if you give up prematurely.

Kitologist Leland Toy, who won numerous awards for his kites before his death in 1992, advised in his book *Flight Patterns*: "You must go out and fly your creations. Some will leap from your hands to soar up to the heavens, others may flop at your feet and lie there like a beached whale...every successful flight...will increase your confidence, and with each mistake you will know what to do next time."

Fear of Being Different

Whatever you do, there will always be someone to criticize you. Beatrice Potter of Jemima Puddleduck, Peter Rabbit and Squirrel Nutkin fame, advised that one should not be "too much afraid of the public for whom I have never cared one tuppeny-button....Most people after one success are so cringingly afraid of doing less well that they rub all the edge off their subsequent work."

Daring to be different is a risk; not daring to be different is a cruncher. Being different, simply for the sake of being different, is pointless. Being different is not a guarantee of creativity. It is, however, an integral ingredient if that difference adds to the value of the creative form, act or statement. Many people are habitually distrustful of those inside or outside their midst who stand out as different. Ironically, the same societies that condemn creators for behaving differently, will eagerly make use of their innovations, once they have gained public acceptance.

> To be great is to be misunderstood.
>
> *Ralph Waldo Emerson, American essayist & poet*

It truly takes strength to allow yourself to see things differently, or to be different, for being an *other*—any kind of other—invites group censorship, and even ridicule. It takes courage to be different and courage is synonymous with creativity. "The word *courage* in my title," said psychoanalyst and professor Rollo May of his book *The Courage to Create*, "refers...to that particular kind of courage essential for the creative act. This is rarely acknowledged in our discussions of creativity and even more rarely written about." It is "the capacity to move ahead *in spite of despair.*"

MacArthur Foundation Fellowship winner Peter Sellars is not afraid of ridicule. This talented man—genius perhaps—who at age twenty-six was made the director of the American National Theater at the Kennedy Center in Washington D.C. and who a few years later was the artistic director of the Boston Shakespeare Company at the Los Angeles Festival, has not been afraid to interpret familiar operas in extremely different ways. He has dared himself to update Mozart, Gilbert and Sullivan, and Shakespeare, for example, even though his detractors have viewed him as a gimmicky upstart.

In her book *Uncommon Genius*, writer Denise Shekerjian examined the creative impulses of some forty winners of the MacArthur Award, including Sellars and child psychiatrist Robert Coles, who taught literature rather than medicine at Harvard and who had written more than fifty books. Many of Coles' peers thought him crazy when, instead of following an orthodox path in medicine, he traveled the United States, South Africa, Northern Ireland, Nicaragua, Northern Canada, Brazil, Poland, Southeast Asia, listening to the questions of children, which were later recorded in his *The Spiritual Life of Children*, the eighth and final volume of his thirty-year, Pulitzer Prize-winning study. It took courage to choose phenomenological inquiry, which he said in Europe was a "well-respected tradition," as opposed to the "overwrought generalizations" of some of his peers.

Courage is also the capacity to allow yourself to be regarded as different. It takes courage to feel alienated, misjudged, alone. The more novel an idea, the more hostile and suspicious its reception. Creative people must be prepared to be regarded as eccentric. They also have to have the courage to make the results of their creativity known, to risk being called *crazy*. "I am never asked where I get my interesting or effective or clever or fascinating ideas," Isaac Asimov said. "I am invariably asked where I get my *crazy* ideas."

Blinkered Thinking

"The past went that-a-way," observed Canadian educator Marshall McLuhan. Something *that* obvious needs to be pointed out because so many people remain trapped in the past. Many people are unable to accept the *presence* of the present. Many wear blinkers, living their lives in bondage to the past—to routines, to repertoires, to rules, to trying to be perfect—past perfect. They set boundaries around their thinking. They welcome restrictions and accept limitations uncritically, because it is secure to remain within given parameters rather than be challenged to traverse them.

Some people believe they have a written contract with every plan they have made. They become fixed on the route they have chosen, even though there might be better ways of achieving a goal, even though their original plan might in the end lead to an adequate solution that is not necessarily the best one.

They have a fixed way of looking at the world and prematurely censor or eliminate potentially good ideas. They do not recognize their hunches, nor do they experiment or embark on creative adventures. They become rigid and lead lives that are planned and bland. Their daily activities and

> Even a cat can cross your plans.
> *Yiddish proverb*

> Any plan is bad which is not susceptible to change.
> *Bartolommeo de San Concordio, Florentine painter & writer*

thinking processes are repetitive. If, for any reason, they are unable to follow their plans, they are not equipped with the thinking skills necessary to reroute. Any alteration of their routine or goals takes an emotional toll.

Many people who fear new possibilities were educated to follow *only* logical but restrictive patterns. A one-answer approach and step-by-step thinking was encouraged. At school they were taught to think vertically, which was useful and dependable. Lateral or divergent thinking was frowned upon. History was taught in *History Class,* economics in *Economics,* art in *Art,* music in *Music* and literature in *Literature.* Although there were some unavoidable crossovers between these vertical categories, there were insufficient linkages between subjects so naturally connected.

Such people emerged from the school system resistant to new ideas or even to enquiring further about what these ideas had to offer. They tended to overvalue the ideas they already had and disapproved of people who had many different ways of looking at things. They correlated many ideas with instability.

Horses wear blinkers to shut off their side views so they do not become frightened or distracted. There are people who obsessively wear blinkers because they are fearful of alternatives, of ambiguity and of new ideas.

A blinkered existence prevents people from capturing the fleeting images and subtleties around them, bringing them to a stability and forming, perhaps, something new. People who only look back to look forward, and never sideways, middleways, under or over, have perspectives that are primarily linear and therefore blinkered. They miss the extraordinary in the ordinary and the ordinary in the extraordinary, for they fail to look at things as they are, but instead see them as vertical connections to what was. Habitually, such people overlook the specificity, and therefore the uniqueness of what they encounter. Instead, their perceptions are homogenized and unoriginal. The fear that necessitates blinkered thinking is a creativity cruncher.

Horses might need flaps sometimes, but we don't. In fact, many of us need to think laterally or divergently more often than we do, because blinkered thinking impedes our advancement and prevents us from reaching a broad understanding of events and issues.

Negativity

Negative people carry a convenient account of what hasn't worked in the past for themselves and for others, and superimpose this ever-available list of problems on emerging ideas, fixating on similarities and ignoring differences. Superrealists, who refuse to see the positive in anything new and not under their control, are creativity crunchers, not only to themselves, but to others as well. They dampen creative thought with negative admonitions and cautionary advice.

> In every work of genius we recognize our own rejected thoughts.
>
> **Ralph Waldo Emerson, American poet & essayist**

They do not encourage new thoughts to develop further, be accepted or rejected, according to their efficacy. Fun, exploration and possibility are not part of their working vocabulary.

Negativity stems from the "no" voices in our heads: the *thought patrols*. These voices of premature judgment are a combination of our own (derived from years of fear and habit) and those of others which have invaded our minds and become our inner censors. New ideas are condemned as soon as they surface, lest they disturb established patterns of thought. "Get all the negative people out of your life," author and visionary Ray Bradbury cautioned in a 1987 lecture. "They're their own funeral."

Negative people do not stay open to new ideas. They allow prophesies to become self-fulfilling. Not only do they impose these prophetic and curtailing visions of doom on themselves, but on others as well, directing futures from their limited and fearful perspectives. They give advice, which is negative, simplistic and often, erroneous, because the "no" voices in their heads preclude thoughtful investigation.

It is hard to argue with negative people because they are generally convinced they are right. The best thing to do is to listen and then follow your hunch and not theirs. You could heed poet, song writer and cartoonist Shel Silverstein's poem *Listen to the Mustn'ts* in which he advised his young readers to listen to all the negatives—the mustn'ts, shouldn'ts, impossibles,—but know "anything can be."

You could also heed the advice of the Magimagician in Juster Norton's *The Phantom Tollbooth* when he said that he often found "that the best way to get from one place to another is to rub everything out and begin again." That is just what you need to do in order to create. You need to erase past records of failure from your mind, at least for a period of time, and pay attention to what is in front of you. In other words, you need to remove your stock of negativity. In this way, you can make the known suddenly seem strange and inviting, and therefore worthy of a new look.

Dogmatism

Exceedingly fearful of the ideas of others, dogmatic people cling fiercely to their own. It is impossible to disagree with them. The intensity of their beliefs silences any opposition. Their need to be right is often accompanied by a fanatical fervor. They forcefeed you with their opinions. It is hard to be creative when you work with such people. The strength of their convictions often dominates and crushes your own inspirations. It is even harder to be creative if you are such a person, for then you are closed to any stimulation, any personal intuition. Dogmatic people are only secure with their own ideas, which they believe are unquestionably correct.

Doubt is courageous; dogma is cowardly. Dogmatic people are ineffective thinkers who have a limited schema upon which to draw. Medical doctor and psychologist Edward de Bono, who has written extensively on lateral thinking, says "the purpose of thinking is to collect information and to make the best possible use of it" and that is precisely what dogmatic people do not do. They are poor

> Dogmas always die of dogmatism.
>
> **Annis Nin, Paris-born American writer**

gatherers of information because their belief in their own correctness blinds them to other possibilities and leaves them, generally, ill-informed.

In countries where people are intellectually passive, dogmatic people are able to be leaders. They can promote collective ideological thinking with ease and forbid any forms of questioning. In countries which encourage individualism on the other hand, they have a difficult time. It is hard to impose an opinion on people who prefer to form their own. Charles De Gaulle, military leader and president of France from 1959 to 1969, once jokingly asked, "How can anyone govern a nation that has two hundred and forty six different kinds of cheese?"

Solution-Bound

Russian writer Alexander Solzhenitsyn observed, "In Russia when you ask questions, you may come to an unfortunate conclusion." This might no longer be applicable to Russia today, but it certainly is to many countries in the world. In the United States, at this point in time, it is safe to ask questions. Yet many people fear if they do so, they will appear ignorant. Instead of asking questions, they tend to seek instant solutions that do not stimulate deeper, more experimental and creative thinking, or lead to a choice of ideas.

An expectation of quick solutions abounds in America because it is associated with quick achievements. Answers are synonymous with winning. There is a need to win in everything, and that need to win can sacrifice truth. When interviewed by Iranian philosopher Ramin Jahanbegloo in 1992, British philosopher and writer Isaiah Berlin commented that "the very idea that you can even in principle find solutions to all questions is absurd."

It is important to doubt and to expect truth. Question as much as you want because question generation will lead to idea generation, which in turn will lead to opportunity generation.

Even if, after sufficient questioning, you reach an excellent answer, it is important to know that other developments might arise in the future. You might then be faced with more questions that might lead to yet better answers. A one-answer approach is about guarantees of answers. It is about quick solutions. A many-answered one is about possibilities and depth.

It takes courage to postpone a solution and to venture into both emotional and intellectual areas that still beg definition, or which might never be easily defined. It is not necessary to characterize everything, because some areas are not at all that easy to pinpoint. It is important not to resist ambiguity, and not fear permitting yourself or others the freedom to journey, independently, into the unknown.

> Freedom from the desire for an answer is essential to the understanding of a problem.
>
> **Jiddu Krishnamurti, Indian theosophist**

Not everything has one easy answer. Not everything is obvious or controllable, right or wrong. Chaos exists, but, within its ambiguity, new and exciting forms are perceivable. In the indeterminacy of fluid and hazy darkness, we can draw upon our hunches, our primary impulses, and combine this in new ways with the logical and the rational. Ambiguity is a challenge for cognitive adventure and an opportunity to perceive things freshly. Creative people allow uncensored perception and are open to examining areas that do not have tidy resolutions. They risk venturing beyond their conscious awareness into the irrational. They risk not having an instant solution.

Rule-Bound

Situations alter. Until recently, wage-earners left their homes to go to work. That was by and large the *rule* of the day. They took private transport, parked in garages or used public transportation to reach a central location—their office, factory, store or school. People who did not leave their homes to go to work and yet provided for their families were regarded as odd.

Today many providers work at home. The old rules of workplace and dress code no longer apply. Technological developments have revolutionized previous ways of doing business. Computer technology and changes in corporate thinking have altered the concept of offices so drastically that many of them are now located miles away from the central headquarters—in residential areas. People have become technologically connected rather than physically, and spatial proximity is no longer a prerequisite for doing business.

> To rest upon a formula is a slumber that prolonged, means death.
>
> Oliver Wendell Holmes Jr., U.S. Supreme Court Justice

Many of the representatives you speak to during business hours, even those from large companies, might well work from desks in the corners of their living rooms or bedrooms. They might be siting on the edge of their beds attached to keyboards and dressed (you hope) in shorts or sweat suits. They are often in distant countries. The rules have changed, and there could be benefits: less traffic, less pollution and more flexibility. These are new alternatives. We have gone full circle since the industrial revolution, and, increasingly, both fathers and mothers once again work from home.

It is important to challenge rules and ask, "Says who?" You need of course, to *know* the rules, but being unquestioningly bound by them can interfere with original thinking. Rules should be overruled when, instead of serving a purpose, they begin to hamper individual creativity, freedom and safety. Rules need to be investigated critically and tested. How did we arrive at this rule? Who invented it? Was it useful? Is it *still* useful? Is it indeed beneficial or does it exist simply because it has been mindlessly or fearfully accepted? If the rules are redundant, obsolete, senseless and even false, we can break them. It is especially important to disregard them if they have begun to hinder our creativity and independent thinking.

Role-Bound

Today in the United States as well as many other countries, there are considerably fewer gender and age constraints on vocational and avocational interests than even a decade ago. Historically, however, there have been differences in what society expected from males and females. Societal definitions of gender roles were passed from generation to generation. Schools, among other groups, promoted educational curricula geared to maintaining these roles. Children, and hence adults, were conditioned into these gender roles by identification, imitation and education, and were fearful of stepping out of them. Very often, opportunities for creative exploration were lost because people had been educated to be role-bound.

Gender roles were once so emphatically defined in the United States that in the 1930 health and home encyclopedia *Vitalogy* (which in its forward assured "an intelligent and discriminating public" that the book would prove "an

> There is no book-hater like a Little League coach. But indeed all the creative arts are obnoxious to the manly ideal, because at their best the arts are pursued by uncompetitive and essentially solitary people.
>
> **Paul Theroux,**
> A *Being a Man*@

> To play the victim today, is in the least ridiculous... I never divide the human souls. They are the same.
>
> **Oriana Fallaci,**
> **Italian novelist & journalist**

instrument of constant usefulness and a possession of inestimable and never-failing value") physician E.H. Ruddock advocated: "Every son of wealth should learn a trade or calling; every daughter of affluence should graduate as a housewife."

"You can't be serious—a doll for boys?" The idea horrified many people when Stanley Weston first conceived G.I. Joe in the early sixties. Of course it wasn't a doll, it was explained, but an action soldier with a remarkable array of clothes and accessories—uniforms, weapons, bandages, even enemies and a G.I Joe Nurse.

Weston's fifty-two dollar investment soon made him $100,000 when he sold it to Hassenfeld Brothers (which later became known as Hasbro), who, thirty years later, had sold $2.6 billion of G.I. Joe products. Within a short time, it had become a best-selling children's toy—even girls had bought it.

Girls, of course, bought Barbie, too, and in astounding numbers since she was first introduced in 1959. Her wardrobe was feminine, theatrical and seductive. But roles change with the times and toy manufacturer Mattel faced complaints when the company programmed a Barbie doll to say, "Math class is tough." She no longer says that. That statement was removed from her repertoire. Instead, there was a white-coated Dr. Barbie with a different set of accessories: a doctor's kit, stethoscope and a newborn infant.

Dream Deprivation

Loss of Fantasy, Loss of Self

> There are vast realms of
> consciousness still undreamed
> of vast ranges of experience,
> like the humming of unseen harps,
> we know nothing of, within us.
>
> **D.H. Lawrence,**
> **"Terra Incognita"**

Severance from Night Dreams

At night we leave our waking world and enter one of dreams. We enter a world in which we are the creators, and the dreamscape is of us. Our dreams occur spontaneously. They are fed by reality and combined with the unconscious, linked perhaps to some great store of accumulated knowledge of which we are barely aware. In our dreams we surrender and connect with subterranean emotions and energies that have come from—somewhere.

English novelist and essayist, mystic and cultural critic Aldous Huxley believed that most dreams are the dramatically symbolic stories of instinctive urges and conflicts "thwarted by a disapproving conscience or a fear of public opinion." In dreams, our private selves escape from public demands. During the day, we drift in and out of daydreams, keeping one eye on reveries and one eye on our world. Unfortunately, we pay insufficient attention to these dreams. We have been taught not to be dreamers because realism is synonymous with maturity and an organized, responsible life.

Dreams feed us, and we feed our dreams. They are us. Symbolic images occur in our dreams, which, although not fully understandable, are worthy of attention as sources of information. Dreams vary. Some are visual, some verbal. Some are vague, endoceptual feelings or blends of feelings, hard to translate accurately into words. A great deal of unconscious cognition is transformed into representational forms when we dream, and as Carl Jung observed, "The dream calls our mind's attention to the body's instinctive feeling."

Novelist and lecturer Robert Moss sees dreams as creative experiences and adventures. "Dreams can be magic carpets," he observed. They can be "a road to our creative source… our dreams alert us to purposes and possibilities beyond the ego's waking agenda." He advises people to capture their dreams by recording them as soon as they awaken from sleep so that they, "the ultimate authority" on their own dreams, do not lose valuable material that fades so quickly. According to Moss, many individuals have credited their inventions to dreams. Friedrich Kekule dreamed of a serpent swallowing its tail and finally grasped the molecular structure of benzene. The structure of the atom was conveyed to Nobel Prize winner Nels Bohr via his dreams, while a nightmare stimulated Elias Howe to invent the modern sewing machine.

> Many characters have come to me…in a dream, and then I'll elaborate from there. I always write down all my dreams.
>
> **William Burroughs, American author**

"Some unseen collaborator"—that's who Scottish writer Robert Louis Stevenson somewhat modestly saw as being worthy of the literary praise which *he*, instead, received for his writing. He regarded the "Little People" in his dreams (who never even told him of their aims) as the real creative force behind his work. They were the ones who gave him "stories piece by piece, like a serial."

These people paid attention to the content of their dreams. Most of us do not examine this huge source of available, indefinable material. We do not employ our secondary processes, that is, our analytical skills to work with this valuable, primary matter. Nor do we try to capture and understand these vague, volatile and difficult-to-remember images. Sadly they are lost, wasted, because a dream dreamt can only become a creation when it is made visible to both us and others—that is, to an audience. Instead, we dream dreams and then disconnect.

We are not in the habit of trying to understand our dream world. Nor do we take it seriously or attempt to connect to a wealth of dream material. Oblivious to its potential, or fearful of embarking on a journey into the unclear and difficult-to-explain areas of our minds, we neglect an important part of our creativity. We do not understand that creativity is the result of the unity of both the conscious and unconscious.

Severance from Daydreams

Dreams need not only occur when we are asleep. They also can be created in our conscious mind. These might be dreams of what we want for the future, expressions of deep desires and aspirations. These daydreams, these uncensored fantasies, are our rehearsals for life. Many of the choices we make can be based on them. In daydreams we audition: for the job interview, for important discussions, for roles in alternate lives. We audition in private, unafraid of the judgment of others, of being told to "get real."

Our creative desires and expressions can be found in our daydreams. Jerome Singer, professor of psychology, proposed that, although some daydreams may simply be diversions, others "may be more than wishful explorations. They may indeed be useful....They may suggest new and alternative ways of dealing with situations."

We need to review our daydreams. Many are valuable and enriching. Singer observed that as humans we have the potential to be enriched and that daydreaming is "a fundamental means of such enrichment." These daydreams often direct us. They are our visions and hopes. Some people manage to cling to their dreams, no matter what. At times, they might put them on hold when other realities claim their attention, but they return to them as soon as they are able.

Daydreams are the rivers that flow through our lives, sometimes swiftly taking us along, other times meandering, sometimes barely moving, risking stagnation. To people connected to their needs and hence to themselves, these rivers run constantly throughout their lives. They are the dreams of their futures, dreams of fame, of success, of love. They exclude sobering and stultifying practicalities such as years of hard work, rejection, financial sacrifice, illness, crying babies and interrupted sleep. We are fed by our daydreams, and, if we pay attention to them, we will learn more about our yearnings. We will recognize the private, unverbalized areas within us.

Severance from Self

We meet ourselves in our dreams, but many of us are not aware of this or that we are more than one self. We are many selves, the ones molded for public consumption, varying according to with whom we are conversing, and with what we hope to achieve, and the other, yearning-to-be self, almost snuffed out, barely inhaling its own selfhood, smothered by the expectations—of others and ourselves.

Sometimes, that other self surfaces unexpectedly and presents us with an alternate self, one we have barely taken the time to know. Our real self is contained within the many selves of our dreams, just as our real self is contained and suppressed in the selves we present to others daily. In literature, we have come across themes of the double. Oscar Wilde's *The Picture of Dorian Gray* or Robert Louis Stevenson's *The Strange Case of Dr. Jekyll and Mr. Hyde* both deal with the *doppelganger*, German for the "double goer" or "double walker." In Ancient Egypt, *ka* was man's exact counterpart, even having the same walk and clothes.

As Pulitzer-Prize winning writer Douglas R. Hofstadter said in his book *The Mind's I*, "It is a common myth that each person is a unity… with a will of its own. Quite the contrary, a person is an amalgamation of many subpersons all with wills of their own."

> Once, my spirit went to Miami for a weekend, and once it was arrested for trying to leave Macy's without paying for a tie. The fourth time, it was actually my body that left my spirit.
>
> **Woody Allen,**
> A*Without Feathers*@

Severance from Childhood

The richness of fantasy is as much a prerequisite in adult life as it is in childhood. It is an essential ingredient of creativity. According to Swiss psychologist Jean Piaget, make-believe is an important aspect of children's normal developmental experiences, facilitating the accommodation and assimilation required in the development of their thinking and coping skills. Jerome L. Singer believed that fantasy is one of the most important ways a child "gradually integrates the complex external environment into a set of organized memories." Although Singer said make-believe is internalized and becomes largely private imagery roughly between the ages of

> The child in me is delighted, the adult in me is skeptical.
>
> Saul Bellow,
> upon receiving the 1976 Nobel Prize for literature

six and thirteen, he believes it is important for it not to disappear entirely. It needs to continue into adult life because the ability to daydream is a significant adaptive skill. Mental exploration and playfulness are essential for creativity.

Just as children are severed from aspects of childhood at too young an age by many intrusions, so adults are removed even further from the children they once were, simply because they are adults and are expected (by themselves and others) to behave accordingly. They are distanced from their fantasies, their dreams and daydreams, and from their creativity.

Creativity should be an ongoing process throughout life, and therefore ageless. Yet, demands interfere. Critical expectations, according to Betty Edwards, author of *Drawing on the Right Side of the Brain,* retard adults' ability to express themselves in their drawing, and in fact, leave most adults unable to draw beyond the level of a nine- or ten-year-old. This is because children of this age have a need for realism and therefore distance themselves from their own creative perceptions.

The desire of adults to be realistic above all else, distances them from the valuable playfulness of childhood. They lose that freshness of vision, and the openness and gullibility that first took place in childhood and was such an important aspect of their creativity.

The seeds of creativity were there in the child. There was a barely containable curiosity, a desire to explore, to discover things and try them out, to attempt to do things differently. While playing on their own or with friends, they created entire universes.

There are adults, too, who continue to create universes throughout their lives, be it in science, in business, in music, and, as was the case with Walt Disney, in entertainment and art. Although he is no longer alive, millions of people annually experience the magic of his kingdoms—in the movies, on television or in Disney theme parks inhabited by pirates, sharks, the Abominable Snowman, Donald Duck, Goofy and Minnie Mouse.

Millions of people worldwide have also enjoyed the animation of Hanna-Barbera. William Hanna and Joseph Barbera produced animated entertainment together for more than fifty years. They gave the world *Huckleberry Hound, Yogi Bear, The Flintstones, The Jetsons, Speed Buggy, Loopy De Loop, Dirty Dawg* and the *Smurfs*, to name only a few of the two hundred plus animated series that have been seen regularly on television since the mid-nineteen-fifties. In 1989, Hanna at age seventy-seven, and Barbera, age seventy-eight, were at work on yet another commission, this time from Turner Broadcasting System, a Tom and Jerry cartoon series. Thirty years previously, they had made their last theatrical Tom and Jerry for MGM.

The ability to combine an adult perspective with a childlike vision is evident in the best of children's stories and illustrations. "My writing is a collaboration between my adult self and my child self," said writer Beverly Cleary, who has created characters such as Henry Huggins, Ralph S. Mouse, Otis Spofford and Ramona Quimby. "Henry Huggins came out of the neighborhood of my childhood."

The imaginary worlds of childhood mature into the sophisticated fantasies of writers such as Gunter Grass and Tom Robbins. While Grass, who has written extraordinarily imaginative works such as *The Tin Drum* and *Local Anaesthesia*, assessed himself as "childlike like most writers," writer

John Irving saw Grass's unique view of the world as a result of both his ability to remain forever young and an extraordinary imagination. "He does not distort history; he out-imagines it," said Irving. "He exercises no discernable restraint on the mischief of his imagination."

Many writers cultivate their childlike capacity for playfulness and whimsy. "I was born with an active fantasy life which I refused to give up," said Tom Robbins, author of books such as *Skinny Legs and All, Even Cowgirls get the Blues* and *Jitterbug Perfume*. Imagination is something you need to nurture he observed, by not allowing other distractions to deaden it, and that is what Robbins did. He fostered his imagination and lived in it and "never watched TV, the archenemy of imagination." Instead, he "grew up on radio" allowing his own mind to elaborate the scenes.

Prerequisites for Creativity

The Final Ingredients

> I trust in inspiration,
> which sometimes comes
> and sometimes doesn't.
> But I don't sit back waiting for it.
> I work every day.
>
> *Alberto Moravia,*
> *Italian novelist*

Stock-Taking

Once you have examined the familial, educative, social and political influences on your life and identified any obstacles they might have caused in the development of your creative thinking, it is useful to examine yourself, honestly. Taking stock of yourself is important. The final ingredients necessary for you to create, reside within you:

- ▼ How do you approach your work?
- ▼ What is your attitude to work?
- ▼ How hard do you strive?
- ▼ Do you take risks in your thinking?
- ▼ Is your work and your interest the same?
- ▼ Different?
- ▼ Are you fortunate enough to be passionately interested in what you do?
- ▼ Are you eager to embrace new projects?
- ▼ Do you then pursue them energetically until their conclusion?
- ▼ Are you dedicated?
- ▼ Serious?
- ▼ Honest with yourself?
- ▼ Fragile?

▼ Negative?

▼ Fearful?

▼ Resistant to new ideas?

▼ Are you receptive to your hunches?

It is essential to identify all hunch crunchers. You need to examine your work processes and know whether you vacillate, procrastinate, deliver on time, only eventually or seldom. There are many factors during the work process that prevent you from reaching your creative potential. It is important for you to examine what stands in the way of you and that finished product. You need to *know* yourself.

A Concept Is Not Enough

No book will jump off a shelf and request your attention. No idea mounted on a white steed will leap through a window and exclaim, "Take me! I'm yours!"

Passivity is a cruncher. Owning ideas requires work. If people have not substantially participated in the development and production of ideas, they do not have a right to them—unless they're lucky enough to convince someone they have. Few ideas are totally original. What is original, is what they *become* during and after the creative process.

There are many people who become stuck at the conceptual stage, who confuse creativity with simply having an idea, or who believe that creativity is absorbed, somehow, through osmosis by being in the right place and among the right people. There are also those who believe that all it takes to be creative is to announce, emphatically, that they have a *great concept*. It generally doesn't take long before such people are considered irrelevant to a project and dismissed, unless, of course, they're lucky.

Success is about what comes *after* an idea. It's about hard work. There are no shortages of ideas; there are shortages of doers. Hollywood script consultant Linda Seger says that it takes five years, on average, for "experienced writers with a workable script and good contacts," to reach the filming stage. It takes longer, she says, for new writers. You have to pay dues, and you have to be "very, very patient."

> Talent is a mastery of quantity: talent doesn't write one page, it writes three hundred.
>
> **Jules Renard, French writer**

An inability to go beyond the hunch is a creativity cruncher. Remaining forever in the conceptual stage is also unproductive. There is no substitute for the perseverance involved in taking ideas and turning them into realities. Hard work, therefore, must accompany ideas. It is a prerequisite. So is talent, energy, tenacity, intelligence and sacrifice.

Creative people proceed beyond the endoceptual and conceptual stages. The primary process produces fragments (which in themselves can be whole); the secondary process voluntarily accepts, incorporates or rejects these for both logical and aesthetic reasons. Sometimes, primary materials become part of new wholes. Sometimes they are aborted because they are no longer relevant. Creative people do not only have inspirations; they also transform them into something communicable. They *make something* of their inspirations.

Some people, motivated by results, will hastily accept an *expedient* form of conveying the idea, thus reducing its creative potential, while a truly creative individual will search persistently for and struggle toward a structural *ideal* for the concept. Such an individual is not satisfied with short cuts, with compromise or collusion with those in power. They will also not be satisfied with imitation. The concept will have to be developed into its best form possible before it is pronounced ready. The road from concept to creativity is long, arduous and rocky.

Nobody suddenly becomes an expert at something. A specific ability is of course required, but so are emotional strength, knowledge, experience, discipline and tenacity. Creative people have an ability to see their work through, even if, at times, circumstances force them to slow down on the execution. They create *regularly*.

The need to focus on their work is ever-present, even when other realities compete for their time. For creative people, work is not a means of passing time or simply a route to financially successful lives. It is their life. Even if their family commitments are of paramount importance, so is their work. Therefore they try to nurture their families as well as their own passions—somehow.

> He that would thrive
> Must rise at five.
> He that hath thriven
> May lie still till seven.
>
> **John Clarke,**
> **17th century writer**

There are passive stages as well as energetic and even frantic periods during the creative process. There are times when creative people need to immerse themselves entirely in the problem at hand and simply think, and other times when they have to work at an accelerated pace in order to capture and develop their impressions before those particular feelings dissipate. They can never be resistant to overwork.

Yet, there are times when people can work too hard, when they simply do not know when to stop. They can cease to see the total picture or become distracted and unable to focus on their work. When this occurs, not only do they become debilitated by their anxieties, but they lose touch with that fleeting emotion that stimulated the enterprise in the first place—that hunch.

A great deal of wasted energy accompanies anxiety. It is exhausting and unproductive. There are times when it is necessary to put the work away for a long or short period of time and try to gain a new perspective, that is, hope to see it again with fresh eyes. Becoming involved in something different for a while helps you achieve distance and permits objective analysis. There are times, however, when you simply have to admit that something is unworkable.

Purpose and Commitment

Isaac Asimov, who produced a huge quantity of work before he died in 1992, knew his purpose so clearly that he once remarked, "If my doctor told me I had only six months to live, I wouldn't brood. I'd type a little faster." He said that the one requirement for him to write was "to be awake." For him a concept was not enough.

Creative people have a sense of purpose, which propels them to take a hunch from its vague, endoceptual origins, to a communicable completion. A theme constantly runs through their lives, one that is sometimes fully in focus, other times vague and peripheral but always within summoning distance. Other realities might compete with it at times, but the theme never abdicates its significant position.

The theme in the life of the creative person is always there, malleable, but connected to its original impulse. The adherence to theme, to purpose, to completion, is what makes the lives of creative people harder, yet passionately

> Great minds have purposes, others have wishes.
>
> **Washington Irving,
> writer and statesman**

richer than the lives of others. The sacrifice of hours of free time, social interaction and financial gain are imperative if the work in progress is to be perfected. It is their purpose which guides them through years—sometimes—of relative isolation. The joy of the work transcends the sacrifice.

It is this sense of purpose that directs the education of the creative person, the acquisition of knowledge, techniques, emotional strength, intensified curiosity and dependable schematic experiences from which to draw. Creative individuals are sustained by this purpose through years of hard work, despair, insecurity, development, self-questioning and directional modifications. They do not sit back and wait for the project to occur. Instead, they risk putting their whole selves into their work, often with grim discipline and singlemindedness of purpose, but always— even when they feel vulnerable—with the belief in the value of what they are hoping to achieve.

These people are committed to their work. This commitment can be so all-encompassing and draining that creative individuals have to remember continually to believe in themselves and constantly be moved by an inextinguishable desire to create something that only months or years of work and rework will place in its best possible form. They have to be prepared to work in areas unknown and hazy, and take chances until the work finally exists in its clearly decipherable, alive and energetic form.

Most enterprises that eventually become significant take years to complete. The game *Monopoly* for example, was anything but an overnight success. It took many years for it to become an international best seller. Parker Brothers initially rejected the game (based on the 1904 *Landlord's Game*) that unemployed engineer Charles Darrow had brought to them. First, he had to publish the game himself and establish its position in the marketplace *before* Parker Brothers bought the rights to it and subsequently sold millions.

Sacrifice

Sacrifice goes with creativity, sometimes at the expense of self-preservation. Creative people are generally short of time for themselves (and others) but somehow make time for their work. Often, therefore, they lack sleep.

"There is this nausea, this fatigue, that writing costs me," Oriana Fallaci told *Boston Globe* staff journalist Patricia Smith in an interview. She had recently completed *Inshallah*, a nearly six-hundred-page novel. "I hate the motionlessness," she said. "You see no people, you don't see the sky, you don't see the sun, you don't see the rain...when your book is finished you have this need for life, for moving. Writing is such a sacrifice in that sense. You live in solitude."

Self-preservation is important and intelligent—to a degree. Therefore, if certain things take a grave emotional toll on us, it would be best to avoid them if we can, or if the work is insufficiently important to us. Pampering ourselves unnecessarily is a creativity cruncher. Regret, self-pity, living in the *past perfect* or perceiving ourselves as permanent victims hampers our thinking and arrests any creative development.

> The only thing more tormenting than writing is not writing.
>
> Cynthia Ozick,
> American novelist

Not only will we be tedious, but we will drain both ourselves and others.

Real life is seldom pain-free, and creating and building something worthwhile is hard, hard work. We cannot capture the joy of building and of being creative if we concentrate obsessively on past mistakes and problems, or if we constantly feel pity for ourselves. We have to look forward to the future and enjoy today and our new beginnings for each new day holds exciting promises for creativity.

Passion—Not Flashin'

Truly creative people feel unfulfilled and frustrated unless they can express creatively their inner lives and their relationship to the external world. They are driven to do so by their emotional connection to the stimulus. They experience an urge to originate something of personal significance, to create a vision uniquely their own. Doing so gives their life meaning.

In *A Sketch of the Past,* English novelist Virginia Woolf spoke about her life including "much more nonbeing than being." A great deal of her every day, she said, was "not lived consciously." Contained within her life instead was "a large proportion of this cotton wool, this nonbeing." Many of us can relate to that feeling of nonbeing—periods when we feel unstimulated and unstimulating, periods when we feel dead.

> Technique alone is never enough. You have to have passion. Technique alone is just an embroidered potholder.
>
> **Raymond Chandler, American novelist**

Passion is the emotional trigger that propels creative people to persist in an effort. It supersedes the need for financial or social reward. Creativity is central to the lives of such people; often it is their life. They do not play at creativity. They do not only talk about it. They are not dilettantes who dabble and trifle. They do not have mere flashes of passion. There is nothing superficial in their interest. "Cotton wool" days for them would be days lacking in creative energy, and days of flashin' would be simply days of what psychoanalyst Rollo May calls "escapist creativity, that which lacks encounter."

Lacking an affinity for something we are doing is a creativity cruncher. Sometimes, because of financial pressure, we have to put the work we wish to do on hold or reluctantly become intermittent creators. Very often though, people remain in fields that do not interest them, not only because of financial necessities, but because they have chosen not to find where their passions lie. Instead, they have settled for mechanical and peripheral work lives, lives of noninvolvement, of *cotton-wool nonbeing*.

Joy

If you had to examine the teachers in your life, how many would stand out as memorable, enthusiastic or exciting? How many truly inspired you? Or did you often feel like Sparky (Charles Schulz's alter ego in *Li'l Folks*—who later evolved into Charlie Brown in *Peanuts*) when he whispered to the little girl sitting in the desk in front of him at school: "It goes without saying that my mere presence here indicates I must be out of my mind!"

A belief prevails that an *attitude* toward schoolwork should be joyless. After all, how can anything difficult be enjoyable? How can one learn while having fun? Wouldn't joy suggest playtime and not the serious discipline of work? Is it possible that puritanical sixteenth century influences are still being felt today in education?

> The worst sin—perhaps the only sin—passion can commit is to be joyless.
>
> Dorothy Sayers, British novelist and playwright

In the mid-sixteenth century, writer Hugh Rhodes urged in his *Book of Nurture*, that children should be kept from the "reading of feigned fables, vain fantasies, and wanton stories and songs of love, which bring much mischief to youth." Books produced for children until the end of the seventeenth century, in fact, were nearly all schoolbooks or books of manners or morals, a literature that was aimed at rescuing children from retribution.

Many educators today understand that, if we want children to have positive attitudes toward school, if we want them to feel excited about going on to higher education, we need to make learning, wherever possible, joyful—which is not to be confused with trivial and unchallenging.

Enjoyment of work is important for adults, too. If our every move is deliberate, serious, focused only on attaining perfection, then we banish the joy of surprising discovery and the creativity involved in the exploratory journey. Taking pleasure in our work not only causes it to flow more easily, but it liberates us to generate ideas—spontaneously, rapidly and enthusiastically. Joy is invigorating to oneself and to others, and an intensity of feeling is an important ingredient in the creative process.

Yet people are expected *not* to enjoy their work. There is *supposed* to be a disparity between play and work. It is commonly believed that if something is fun, it cannot possibly be worthwhile. If something comes easily, it should not be regarded as serious or even be respected. Work is seen as a hardship and the routes taken to achieve a goal are expected to be emotionally draining and empty of passion. Fun removes the *work* from work.

Charles M. Schulz, creator of the *Peanuts* comic strip, described in *Charlie Brown & Charlie Schulz* how he has to alter his behavior to give people a visual image they expect of a person at work: "It's hard to convince people when you're just staring out of the window that you're doing your hardest work of the day. In fact, many times when I'm sitting here thinking and therefore really working, I hear the door open and I quickly grab the pen and a piece of paper and start drawing something and so people won't think I'm just goofing off and anxious to have a little chat."

Work and play do complement each other and overlap. A happy, fulfilled person will be less judgmental of new things and more able to be intuitive. Similarly, a happy, secure workforce will be more cohesive and productive. The months and years it takes to bring a work to fruition, though difficult, can also be stimulating and enriching. We should never squander that valuable journey, but try to enjoy it. As writer and philosopher Robert Pirsig observed, "Sometimes it's a little better to travel than to arrive."

Deadlines or Dead Lines?

A deadline means it is time to arrive. The journey has ended. A deadline can be a cruncher or an energizer. It can be an excellent incentive for starting and completing projects. Very often, the attention required to deliver something on time helps individuals focus on their work and eliminate extraneous anxieties. Many people find that being thrust into a no-choice situation is a stimulus for creativity.

Everything else recedes in importance. The time has come to focus unstintingly on the task ahead.

If there is a financial reward because of timely completion, it helps many individuals rid themselves of the guilt of not attending to a family member, for example, or a competing project. The deadline also facilitates in the decision-making process. The work required has to be given immediate attention; there is no alternative. Daily distractions are dispensed with, and what had appeared necessary in a person's routine suddenly become expendable. Little now stands in the way of a project whose time has come.

> He lived a life of going-to-do,
> And died with nothing done.
>
> **James Albery,**
> **British playright**

Some people, however, do not react well to pressure. Instead of giving them the impetus to strive even harder and extend themselves well beyond their usual limits, a deadline imposes an anxiety that interferes with the clarity of their thought processes. They become unnecessarily distracted and therefore unproductive. For such people, a deadline produces dead lines. Only experience will counteract their destructive reactions to the imposition of a time limit. Eventually, they might learn to regard pressure as a challenge and an invitation to start the task *immediately*.

Empathy

Empathy is an important ingredient of creativity. It is an ability some people have to project themselves imaginatively into the heads of others and understand emotions, problems, fears and desires, that, although not their own, either could be or could never be. People can be quite different to the individuals with whom they empathize, but, because judgment does not interfere and imagination is present, they are easily able to step into those individuals' shoes.

Empathetic people see and feel themselves in others because those other experiences and emotions are accessible to them. Involuntarily and without *deliberately* attempting to be empathetic, they simply are. They instinctively understand and intuitively see another's situation.

Writers or actors demonstrate empathetic skills. They dwell within the heads of others and remain in character for as long as is necessary. A good actor, according to Hollywood screenwriter Robert Towne, will "know what (a character is) thinking, and what he is not thinking...An actor brings all of his skills and sensibilities to the role."

> When your tooth aches, you know how to sympathize with one who has a toothache.
> **Chinese proverb**

Novelist Charles Baxter observed that a writer's ability to create convincing characters stems from an ability to be "chameleon-like," to "slip into somebody's skin temporarily and slip out again." Baxter thinks that we all have many potential selves, but writers are more able to free them. "Most of those characters on those pages," he said, "are potential versions of what I might have been."

There are many professions which require empathetic skills. Certainly teaching, doctoring and counseling do, and the interpersonal success of professionals involved in these fields depends largely on their sensitivity to others. Being shoe-bound, that is unable to stand in anybody else's shoes but your own, is a creativity cruncher and indicative of poor intuitive communication.

Connectivity

Knowledge without intuition is dead. It is simply *details*. There are many people who gather details without any intuitive or creative interpretation, and without knowing the difference between the relevant and the trivial. They therefore give over-attention or equal attention to relevant and irrelevant matters, thus minimizing what is really important. Isaac Asimov called these details "bits," and said that we have probably all met detailed people lacking in deductive ability, insight and intuition "who are intensely educated, but who manage to be abysmally stupid, nevertheless. They have 'bits,' but the 'bits' just lie there." These bits are unconnected. Yet creativity is about connectivity.

"My talent concerns connectivity," paleontologist, teacher, essayist and MacArthur award winner Stephen Jay Gould explained to Denise Shekerjian when she interviewed him for her book *Uncommon Genius*. "I can sit down on just about any subject and think about twenty things that relate to it and they're not hokey connections." Somewhat modestly he observed that, although he is not especially well read and really average intellectually, he can *use* everything he has ever read. What he can do is *connect*.

> I very much loved...the feeling of bringing...totally unrelated...areas of my life together as one can in fiction.
>
> **John Cheever,
> American writer**

In *The Act of Creation*, Arthur Koestler called this combining and rearranging of independent and diverse elements or frames of mind "bisociation." Isaac Asimov said it is intelligence that facilitates a creative person intuitively combining the relevant "bits." Some minds, he said, "have greater capacity for dredging the combinations out of the unconscious and becoming consciously aware of them. This results in 'new ideas,' in 'novel outlooks.'"

Once the creative urge goes beyond the hunch, the creative person resorts to many active mental processes and finds unexpected connections. That person has the ability to create new ideas by combining previous experiences with each other, or simply with imagination, that is, with what has yet to be experienced, or with what might never be experienced. Such a person perceives resemblances between things and connects.

If we allow information to exist untouched by our hunches, we simply have details, and this does not contribute to creativity. If we do not connect these details thoughtfully, instinctively and intelligently, we simply have a collection of somewhat meaningless trivia that directs nobody anywhere further. We need to perceive the similarities among things and the differences, and know that if something is similar, it does not necessarily mean it is identical. Our intellectual depth influences whether we are able to distinguish between significant or trivial connections, whether the concepts fit or do not. Our creative ability will connect things easily and rapidly and the connections will make sense, for if they do not, they will be hastily eliminated and other connections will be tried. Our hunches will tell us which combinations are appropriate and which are not.

Adaptability

Life is not static and changes are inevitable. Intelligent people adapt to changes, and creativity helps in their adjustments and in their adaption to their times. Such people are also influenced by the times and influence them in turn with their creativity. For something to be creative, rather than simply different or even bizarre, it must be received, valued and understood by an audience other than oneself. In other words, it needs to connect to that audience. This connection, however, might be limited to an audience of a few because the creator happens to be living in the wrong place perhaps: a country with the wrong emotional, economic, political, social or religious environment.

Alternatively, creative individuals might be living in the right place at the wrong time. They might be *too late* for their times and so their themes have become irrelevant, or they might be *ahead* of their times creatively and therefore unable to interest an audience. This lack of timeliness commonly occurs in science, literature and the arts, as well as in commerce, where very often products or concepts are recognized long after their introduction. This was the case in the early 1970's with Nolan Bushnell, founder of Atari. At first he was unable to interest pinball manufacturers in his game *Pong*, and so had to manufacture it himself. Within three years he sold it to Warner Communications for $28 million. *They* had caught up. By 1982, the sales of Atari had reached $2 billion.

> I am only a public entertainer who has understood his time.
>
> **Pablo Picasso,**
> **Spanish artist**

The naked bodies and wild beasts in the art of children's author and illustrator Maurice Sendak were once considered highly inappropriate for children. Objections were raised to his 1963 book *Where the Wild Things Are*, and the 1970 book *In the Night Kitchen*. *Today* he is revered and emulated, and has, as Michael di Capua of the publishing company Farrar, Strauss & Giroux remarked, "turned the entire tide of what is acceptable, of what is possible to put in children's-book illustration. There is nobody to compare with Maurice."

Sometimes a new regime can rob an economist, an artist, a writer or a politician of his theme and render it redundant. The individual might have had a vested interest in his theme or with a regime or a particular kind of political correctness. A creative and therefore adaptable person should be able to look at a situation as it *was* and as it *has become*, and describe accurately (without partisanship) circumstances as they unfold. Today, more than ever, the need for educated, intelligent, creative, versatile, independent thinking is extremely urgent.

Collaborative Creativity

Because of the grave political, social, and environmental problems we face today, it is essential to work together collaboratively; many *minds* make *light work* as long as these minds belong to intelligent, independent and creative thinkers, and never to those obsessed with hatred. Individuals, groups leaders and their followers, whose sole purpose in life is to blame (or even murder) the *other* are totally devoid of the creative impulse. They hate instead of create. Their need to blame or destroy the *other* has become, tragically, their sole means of self-and-national definition. If they relinquish that hatred, they lose their identity. But creating together implies building, improving, caring, and collaborating *positively*; there is no place for destructive intentions.

> Mass movements have the peculiarity of overpowering the individual by mass suggestions and making him unconscious.
>
> **Carl Jung,**
> **Swiss psychiatrist**

> The trouble with people who live for revenge is that they're never quite sure when they've had it—and so, to be on the safe side, they go on and on, endlessly.
>
> **Peter Ustinov,**
> **British writer & actor**

Before we can become worthwhile contributors to creative collaborations, we need to be able to create alone—to be adept creators. Creative thinking comes with practice, with the experience of being open to ideas which often begin with an intuitive connection to an emotion—before logical thought and analysis succeed. We need to be comfortable with ambiguity, with feeling our way through the creative process, while always remembering that the sense of what we want is critical to authentic production.

Creative people respect their intuitions and transform the vague into the original, thoughtful, or even, brilliant idea or product. Intuition is a major requirement in team work as well. As Isaac Asimov pointed out, "You cannot add non-intuition and form intuition." It is imperative, he stressed, that at the very least, *one* member of the group is intuitive.

Working alone is a valuable route to discovering our creativity, and so is working with others. Even though creativity is largely a solitary process, collaborating with others helps us build up our store of criteria for something to be worthwhile. It gives us other opinions about art, science, politics, global issues, our own ideas and our own work. This can be timely and useful—as long as we have a commitment to our vision which enables us to select the suggestions which advance what we are doing, and reject those which do not. The ability to create and a sense of aesthetics, develop from the joy and pleasure derived from doing something well. By working with others whose work and thoughts have value, we soon learn to recognize quality in ourselves and others, and expect it.

Most creative people's work-life consists of concurrently working independently and together. They usually give their collaborative projects priority because others depend on their contribution and could be delayed if they are tardy. Although most creative people enjoy working alone, and it is essential for them to do so, it does take enormous discipline to spend so many hours by themselves. Working with others, therefore, counteracts and complements the solitariness. But creative people value and need the aloneness and so are continually torn between the need to be isolated and the need to be with others. Allowing collaborative creativity into their lives gives them that added stimulation and the opportunity to work on projects requiring a number of people, the kind of creative enterprises they could never complete on their own.

> No one person can accomplish much if they don't work with others.
>
> Daniel Levinson, Chief Justice

Some creative individuals are able to find almost equal satisfaction working alone and in groups. This is because they have identified, understood, and accepted the different disciplines needed for both kinds of work, and are also able to respect other people's viewpoints. They have the capacity to focus on ideas rather than on their own personal motives, and remain at all times courteous and fair.

> Great discoveries and achievements invariably involve the cooperation of many minds.
>
> Alexander Graham Bell
> Scottish-born
> American Inventor

Experiencing working creatively with others is a particularly important life and career preparation. Today, collaborations of all kinds are in progress. Indeed, creativity is flowing in all directions, breaking barriers by combining so many seemingly disparate disciplines, blending the arts with the sciences and technology, and forming new creative, multitudinous and multinational wholes. People from so many disparate disciplines, even from areas not traditionally regarded as creative, are now needed because their knowledge and insights help develop new forms, the unique works of many.

But of course there can be drawbacks to collaborative creativity: If, for example, there are deadlines or other people to consider, the participants may not dwell (for as long as they need to) in the margins until their ideas have reached their creative potential. They cannot afford the luxury of allowing greater chaos for a longer period of time, but are forced, prematurely, to organize and control the still confusing creative energy within them. Teamwork can interrupt a valuable train of thought or transform a developing idea into something that differs from what was intended, and the result can sometimes be worse for the interference; sometimes it can be better.

Another drawback is an environment that encourages surface penetration—a lack of depth and authentic personal involvement of the participants. Such a collaboration will limit the possibilities of what is being created. Very often, too, if the motivations of individuals within the group are extrinsic and not from a deep source, they will have lower levels of creativity.

In *Making a Good Script Great*, script consultant Linda Seger acknowledged that the rewriting process—the committee approach—common to the movie and television industry, can have a devastating affect on a script. "The farther they get from the original inspirational source," she said, "the more muddled they become. They begin to lose their magic....By the twelfth rewrite, the story is completely different and no one wants to do the film anymore."

Sometimes, too, members of a collaborative group will not express themselves as freely as they would if they created alone because harmony, an immensely important aspect of teamwork, is absent. They are therefore self-conscious or fear derision. Sometimes, an atmosphere of harmony in a work environment is deceptive because the ostensible cooperation can really be a result of suppression—a fear of voicing an alternate opinion and risking criticism.

Committees can be unproductive if they waste time arguing and asserting power. This occurs especially when the ego of any member is in the way, or if an individual within a collaborative group

> I praise loudly,
> I blame softly.
>
> Catherine "The Great",
> Empress of Russia,
> 1729-1796

inhibits others via authoritarian decisiveness. Each participant's attitude and enthusiasm directly affects the end product, but when the group is discordant, the whole becomes less than the parts.

But within the ideal collaborative group, one in which we can celebrate differences and similarities without a need to compete with, denigrate or negate others, and one in which in-depth, creative exploration is paramount, the advantages of working together are enormous. First of all, there is the fun, especially if the emphasis is primarily on experimentation and not on self-congratulation. And furthermore, such a group offers security—a meeting place for creating minds where the unexpected is sought within a safe environment which gives the participants feelings of authenticity and the permission (from themselves) to create. While collaborating, individuals can discover paths that have been either unclear, categorized as belonging to others, or simply beyond their grasps.

Collaboration encourages artistic, scientific, and philosophical communications outside the realm of the participants' everyday experiences, helping them to become not only appreciators, but creators as well. Working with diverse artists makes varied artistic expressions accessible, understandable and even possible. It encourages, even forces group members to go beyond their safe definitions of self, and express themselves artistically in ways they might never have done had they not been part of a collaboration. Group energy brings concepts to actualization and the commitment to the group makes individuals less guilty about creative time. Deadlines have to be honored. All must do their bit if group members are not to be let down. Within the group, too, members might find mentors—people who stimulate and extend their experiences and creativity, and who give them instant feedback and reinforcement. What we learns from observing others at work can improve our own work-styles and techniques.

So why collaborate? Because it can be an enriching detour on the way to individual creativity, or, in fact, the path to individual creativity. Second and third careers have emerged from creative collaborations because of the opportunities to re-invent one's self through trying new things. And very importantly, if we collaborate with others, we can play in unfamiliar areas without being an expert, intrude (with permission and therefore freely) on the territories of others while leaving our labels and our paths behind, and find, perhaps, new and better areas for ourselves. And this is even important for those highly-trained specialists who hide prematurely behind their designations, asserting something different is not for them, when it might be. How can they (or in fact we) know what we do best or enjoy the most, if we don't try new things? Furthermore, we need to know what it *feels like to create* in order to create.

> Later...I was to encounter... inspiring men...writers, thinkers, poets, troubadours of the apocalypse. Each gave me something for my journey: a phrase, a wink, an enigma. And I was able to continue.
>
> **Elie Wiesel,**
> **Nobel Laureate**

Collaborative work can be creatively challenging and satisfying, and it can lead to the development of exciting projects. Although concepts can be seen in very different ways, concept sharing and conveyance between people can be stimulating. In today's world of global terrorism and environmental destruction, stimulating one another to think more penetratingly, more intelligently (as opposed to mindlessly) more creatively and therefore effectively, is essential.

Humor

Humor is an essential ingredient of creativity. It helps when you take chances, are reckless, or make creative leaps which fail. People with a sense of humor see things differently. They recognize the ludicrous in a situation, or the incongruous or comical, and effectively give expression to these perceptions.

In many ways, people with a sense of humor, are often more serious than their earnest counterparts, and are able to differentiate the significant from the insignificant. They instinctively know what to take seriously and what not to take seriously. Humorous people are actually too serious to take themselves seriously, too serious to give unnecessary importance to the trivial.

Humor frees us from conventional ways of thinking and allows us to experiment and make unexpected connections. In fact, the connections humorists make can be quite startling. Entertainer and musician Victor Borge, for example, saw the visual connection between cigarette smoking and elephants when he explained that the keys to his piano were so old and yellow because "the elephant smoked too much."

Humor, like wit, is primarily intellectual in that it encompasses swift perceptions of similarities in seemingly dissimilar things. It puts situations into perspective. Being able to laugh at ourselves frees us to take risks, make mistakes and face the criticism of others. It allows us to illuminate a truth humorously and yet seriously.

Humor can also be an outlet for repression. By means of a joke we can risk saying the unacceptable. Humorous people are spontaneous, able to laugh not only at a joke, but, without editing, instantly provide one. Creating that joke means taking a chance—and volunteering to an audience that direct product of a hunch or of an amusing image. That joke, like any product of your creativity, might work. It might be funny. It might not. It might be plain dumb. That's why humor is risky.

Decision

Indecision can be more stressful than decision. Self-actualizing people make decisions and strive constantly to realize their goals and hence their potential, rather than hide behind their indecision. There comes a time when research has to stop and we have to commit. Eventually we have accumulated sufficient knowledge to go forward, to follow our hunches.

There are many people, however, who, for a variety of reasons, find decision making extremely difficult. Their method for making choices (or not making them) is very different to that of a person such as William Gates, co-founder of Microsoft, who said his business strategy was to "decide where the future lies and bet everything on getting there first."

Indecisive people tend to lead vague, frightened lives of unselected possibilities. They are excessively fearful of making mistakes. Such people do not realize that, if things do not work out, they could try another route.

Then there are others who make decisions too hastily because they are unable to deal with the haziness of many choices. Because of insufficient examination, they often take a wrong approach. They have not been guided by their hunches but by a desire for an

> We know what happens to people who stay in the middle of the road. They get run over.
>
> **Aneurin Bevan,
> Welsh politician**

instant solution. A wrong decision, though costly, might prove useful because it could provide them with the experience to make a better choice next time.

Once we have made sufficient preparation, we need to move on. We have to be sensitive to what *feels* right. Decision-making is about giving ourselves permission to go forward on a journey. It is about giving ourselves the right to pursue a need, to succeed and to make errors. It's about following a *hunch*.

It's Time For Lunch

> Somewhere something incredible is waiting to be known.
>
> Carl Sagan,
> American writer,
> & astronomer

Food for Thought

One fresh Hunch
Two Cups of Intelligence
Two Cups of Talent
Three Cups of Daring
Four Cups of Expertise

Active ingredients:
imagination, persistence,
commitment, purpose,
enthusiasm, humor.

Stir the above together and allow it to simmer for the rest of your life. Don't forget to add a dash of luck.

It's time for lunch. It's time to sit down at a table—at whatever venue you choose—with your hunch. You now have an opportunity to communicate with a very important part of yourself, a part of which you have been generally unaware, a part to which you have not given enough attention.

Your hunch crunchers have been addressed, obstacles identified and many have faded away. They will not pounce on you again—unless you let them. It is now time to enjoy that exciting meeting with the *something* that dwells within you, entice it to life and experience that fusion of both your conscious and unconscious. You are ready to dip into that invaluable resource: your potential.

The dialogue with your hunch will flow effortlessly and unconditionally. There will be no intrusions, for it is now *hunchtime*. Nothing else can impinge on your awareness. You will listen attentively and unjudgmentally to your hunch and ask it many questions. One question will lead to another and another. You will go in surprising directions while you listen. There will be no voices in your head shouting that you are wrong, that you are presumptuous and that you are dumb. You will be impervious to criticism at this stage. It is only you and your hunch, and neither of you is interested in negativity.

> The best kind of conversation is that which may be called thinking aloud.
>
> **William Hazlitt (1778-1830)**
> ***Characteristics in the Manner of Rochefoucault's Maxims***

Together, you will develop your talent and push it beyond what you thought were its limitations. You will work on what comes naturally and what you had never sufficiently respected before: your own creativity. Because you take your hunch seriously, together you will journey to wherever your joint enterprise will lead. Sometimes you will invite others to join you. The routes you follow along the way will be varied, risky and surprising. You will transform ordinary landscape into new forms with unbounded possibilities.

The date with your hunch involves passion, endurance and commitment. It is a journey that leads to self-discovery, an awareness of sounds and the silence of a mind emptied of judgment and then filled differently. At times you will use what already exists and, freed from the constraints of standardized thinking, change it in unexpected ways. At other times you will cause what is in your imagination to come to life.

Creativity is about freedom and boundaries. The new ideas you have created will be relevant and within the parameters of human communication. There will always be strings attached to what you do, but once you have identified and understood them, they need no longer be creativity crunchers.

There is also a vision that guides a creative process that is uniquely your own. Creativity is about the selection of the relevant from the unnecessary. At various stages, your hunches will help you to choose, compare, combine, connect, blend and mend until you have a unity of content and form, an external depiction of your internal vision. Your journey may never be completed. It might always be one of becoming.

So, take your hunch to lunch. Wine and dine it. Listen to it and woo it. If you have more than one hunch, take them all to lunch, together or separately—it all depends on you. If some hunches are disappointing, it doesn't matter. It will not be the first time a lunch date was less satisfying than anticipated. Another hunch at another time will stimulate you to create. Take your hunch to lunch today, and you never know, one day it might take you.

> "We mustn't stop now or we shall be late."
> "Late for what?"
> "For whatever we want to be in time for."
>
> **A.A. Milne**

Text Bibliography

Allen, Woody. "My Speech to the Graduates." In *Side Effects*. London: New English Library, 1981.

Anderson, Hans Christian. *The Diaries of Hans Christian Anderson*. Trans. Patricia L. Conroy and Sven H. Rossel. Seattle: University of Washington Press, 1991.

Arieti, Silvano. *Creativity: The Magic Synthesis*. New York: Basic Books Inc., 1976

Asimov, Isaac. "Those Crazy Ideas." In *The Essay Connection*. 3rd ed. Ed. Lynn Z. Bloom. Lexington: D.C. Heath and Company, 1991.

Atwood, Margaret. "Where is How." *Publishers Weekly* 8 Aug. 1991.

Banville, John. "An Interview with Salman Rushdie "*New York Review of Books* 4 March 1993.

Bettelheim, Bruno. *The Uses of Enchantments: The Meaning and Importance of Fairy Tales*. New York: Knopf, 1976.

Borge, Victor. In *The Big Book of New American Humor*. Ed. William Novak and Moshe Waldoks. New York: HarperPerennial, 1990.

Bradbury, Ray. Lecture at the Phoenix Civic Center, 18 Sept. 1987.

Brady, John. *The Craft of the Screenwriter*. New York: Touchstone, 1982.

Brainard, Dulcy. "Robert Coles." *Publishers Weekly* 16 Nov. 1990.

Brandt, Richard. "The Billion-Dollar Whiz Kid." *Business Week* 13 April, 1987.

Cantor, Eddie. *New York Times* 20 Oct. 1963.

Carver, Raymond. *The Paris Review*, Number 88. New York: 1983.

Coles, Robert. *The Spiritual Life of Children*. Boston: Houghton Mifflin, 1990.

Connell, Christopher. "Teen Carnage." *Associated Press rpt. Scottsdale Progress* 24 March 1993.

Corsini, Raymon J. "George Herbert Mead." *Encyclopedia of Psychology*. Vol. 2. New York: John Wiley & Sons, 1984.

Cousins, Norman. In *The Book of Quotes*. Ed. Barbara Rowes. New York: E.P. Dutton, 1979.

Crystal, David. *The Cambridge Encyclopedia of Language*. New York: Cambridge University Press, 1987.

Davies, Paul. *The Mind of God: Science and The Search for Ultimate Meaning*. London: Penguin Books, 1992.

De Bono, Edward. *Lateral Thinking: Creativity Step by Step*. New York: Perennial Library, Harper & Row, 1973.

De Gaulle, Charles. In *The Book of Quotes*. Ed. Barbara Rowes. New York: E.P. Dutton, 1979.

Devareaux, Elizabeth. "Charles Baxter." *Publishers Weekly* 7 Dec. 1992.

Dillard, Ann. Winokur, Jon. ed. *Advice to Writers*. New York: Pantheon Books.1999.

Edlin, Mari. "Tom Robbins" *Publishers Weekly* 25 May 1990.

Edwards, Betty. *Drawing on the Right Side of the Brain*. Los Angeles: Jeremy P. Tarcher 1989.

Furbank, P.N. *Diderot: A Critical Biography*. New York: Knopf,, 1992.

Gardels, Nathan. "Two Concepts of Nationalism: An Interview with Isaiah Berlin." *The New York Review of Books* 21 Nov. 1991.

Gardner, Michael. *Frames of the Mind: The Theory of Multiple Intelligences*. New York: Basic Books, 1983.

Gelman, Morrie. "Hanna and Barbera: After 50 Years, Opposites Still Attract." *Variety* 12-18 July, 1989.

Gergen, Kenneth J. *The Saturated Self*. New York: Basic Books, 1991.

"G.I. Joe Creator to Mark Doll's 30th with a Yearlong 'Salute'." *The Associated Press repr. The Scottsdale Progress* 8 Feb. 1994.

Gleick, James. *Genius: The Life and Science of Richard Feyman*. New York: Pantheon, 1992.

Goleman, Daniel, Paul Kaufman and Michael Ray. *The Creative Spirit*. New York: Dutton, 1992.

Gregory, Richard L. ed. "George Herbert Mead." *The Oxford Companion to the Mind*. New York: Oxford University Press, 1987.

Guber, Selina S., and Jon Berry. *Marketing To and Through Kids*. New York: Mc-Graw-Hill Book Co., 1993.

Hansen, Sandra. "The Writing Life [on Beverly Cleary]." *Writers Digest* Jan. 1983.

Harper, Lucinda. "Report Suggests All Isn't Well With USA Families." *Wall Street Journal* 29 March 1993.

Havel, Vaclav. "Paradise Lost." *The New York Review of Books* 9 Apr. 1992.

—. *Disturbing the Peace*. New York: Vintage Books, 1991.

—. "Reflections on a Paradoxical Life." *The New York Review of Books* 14 June 1990.

—. "Uncertain Strengths." *The New York Review of Books* 15 Aug. 1991.

Hoffman, Banesh. *Albert Einstein—Creator and Rebel*. New York: The World Publishing Company, 1971.

—"My Friend, Albert Einstein." In *The Longwood Reader*. Eds. Dornman, Edward A. and Charles W. Dawe. Boston: Allyn and Bacon, 1991.

Hofstadter, Douglas, and Daniel C. Dennett. *The Mind's I: Fantasies and Reflections on Self and Soul*. London: Penguin Books, 1981.

Holman, C.Hugh, and William Harmon, *A Handbook to Literature* 6th ed. New York: Macmillan, 1992.

Huxley, Aldous. *The Doors of Perception & Heaven and Hell*. New York: Harper Colophon Books: 1963.

Irving, John. "Gunter Grass: King of the Toy Merchants." *Saturday Review* March 1982.

Jahanbegloo, Ramin. "Philosophy and Life: An Interview [Isaiah Berlin]" *New York Review of Books* 28 May 1992.

Jones, Margaret. "Rage for Recovery." *Publishers Weekly* 23 Nov. 1990.

—. "Getting Away from the 'R' Word." *Publishers Weekly* 5 July 1993.

Joyce, James. *Dubliners*. New York: The Viking Press, 1969.

—. *Stephen Hero*. New York: New Directions Publishing Corp., 1963.

Jung, C. G. *America Facing It's Most Tragic Moment, C. G. Jung Speaking*. London: Thames & Hundson, 1978.

Juster, Norton. *The Phantom Tollbooth*. London: William Collins Sons, 1962.

Kiley, Brian. In *The Big Book of New American Humor*. Eds. Novak, William, and Moshe Waldoks. New York: Harper Perennial, 1990.

Koestler, Arthur. *The Act of Creation*. New York: Macmillan, 1964.

Kosinski, Jerzy. *Being There*. San Diego: Harcourt Brace Jovanovich Inc., 1970.

Lannon, Linnea. "Author [Robert Coles] issues 'Call' to Make World Better." *Arizona Republic* 3 Oct. 1993.

Lasch, Christopher. *Haven in a Heartless World*. New York: Basic Books, 1975.

—-. *Culture of Narcissism*. London: Abacus, 1980.

Lawson, Carol. "Toy Makers See Dollars in Blurring Stereotypes." *The New York Times repr. Scottsdale Progress* 12 Feb. 1993.

"The Learning Revolution." *Business Week* 28 Feb. 1994.

Linder, Leslie transcr. *The Journal of Beatrice Potter, 1881-1897*. New York: Viking Penguin, 1990.

Lucaire, E. *The Celebrity Almanac*. New York: Prentice Hall, 1991.

McGuire, William, and R.F.C. Hull, eds. *C.G. Jung Speaking: Interviews and Encounters*. London: Thames and Hudson, 1978.

Maslow, Abraham H. *Motivation and Personality*. 2nd ed. New York: Harper and Row, 1970.

Mason, Jackie. In *The Big Book of New American Humor*. Eds. Novak, William, and Moshe Waldoks. New York: Harper Perennial, 1990.

May, Rollo. *The Courage to Create*. New York: Bantam, 1976.

Mendelson, Lee and Charles M. Schulz. *Li'l Folks Charlie Brown and Charlie Schulz*. New York: The World Publishing Co., 1970.

Moss, Robert. "What Your Dreams Can Tell You." *Parade* 30 Jan. 1994.

Nabokov, Vladimir. Winokur, Jon. ed. *Advice to Writers*. New York: Pantheon Books.1999.

Pirsig, Robert. *Zen and the Art of Motorcycle Maintenance*. London: Corgi Books, 1976.

Plimpton, Geroge. *The Paris Review*. 7th Series. New York: Penguin 1988.

Plimpton, Geroge. *The Paris Review*. 8th Series. New York: Penguin 1998.

Plunket, Robert. "Garbo, by Any Other Name." *The New York Times Book Review* 30 May 1993.

Postman, Neil. *The Disappearance of Childhood*. New York: Laurel, 1984.

—-. *Amusing Ourselves to Death*. London: Methuen Paperback, 1985.

Rader, Dotson. "How to Live Without Answers." *Parade* 25 Apr. 1993.

Reed, Ishmael. "What's American about America?" In *Ourselves Among Others*. Ed. Carol J. Verburg. Boston: Bedford Books, 1991.

Ripple, R.E. and V. N. Rockcastle. *Piaget Rediscovered*. Ithaca: Cornell Univerity Press, 1964.

Rosten, Leo. *The Joys of Yinglish*. New York: Signet Book, 1992.

Ruddock, E.H. *Vitalogy: An Encyclopedia of Health and Home*. Chicago: Vitalogy Association 1930.

Sapir, Edward. *Language*. New York: Harcourt Brace, 1921.

Seger, Linda. *Making a Good Script Great*. Hollywood: Samuel French, 1987.

Shekerjian, Denise. Uncommon Genius. New York: Penguin Books, 1991.

Short, Robert L. *The Parables of Peanuts*. New York: Harper & Row, Publishers, 1968.

Silverstein, Shel. "Listen to the Mustn'ts." In Where the Sidewalk Ends. New York: Harper Collins, 1974.

Singer, Jerome L. *Daydreaming and Fantasy*. Oxford: Oxford University Press, 1981.

Skynner, Robin, and John Cleese. *Families and How to Survive Them*. New York: Oxford University Press, 1983.

Slonimsky, Nicolas. *Lexicon of Musical Invective*. Seattle: University of Washington Press, 1969.

Smith, Patricia. "Oriana Fallaci." *The Boston Globe*, 5 Jan 1993.

Solzhenitsyn, Alexander. *The Gulag Archipelago*. London: Collins & Harvill Press, 1975.

Sonheim, Amy. *Maurice Sendak*. New York: Twayne Publishers, 1992.

Spiegelman, Arthur. "Science Fiction's Isaac Asimov Dies." *Reuters rpt. The Arizona Republic* 7 April, 1992.

Stern, Sydney Ladensohn, and Ted Schoenhaus. *Toyland. The High-Stakes game of the Toy Industry*. Chicago: Contemporary Books, 1990.

Sternburg, Janet. *The Writer on Her Work*. New York: W.W. Norton, 1980.

Stevenson, Robert Louis. "A Chapter on Dreams." Rpt. in *Dreams and Inward Journeys*. Eds. Marjorie Ford and Jon Ford. New York: Harper & Row, 1990.

Thio, Alex. "George Herbert Mead." *Sociology*. New York: Harper & Row, 1986.

Townsend, John Rowe. *Written For Children*. Middlesex: Penguin Books, 1974.

Toy, Leland. *Flight Patterns*. Scottsdale: Sky High Press, 1987.

Tylor, Sir Edward Burnett. *The Origins of Culture*. New York: Harper Torchbooks, 1958.

Walker, Margaret. Sternburg, Janet. ed. *The Writer on Her Work*. New York: W.W. Norton & Company. 1980.

Wallach, Michael A. and N. Kogan. *Modes of Thinking in Young Children: A Study of the Creativity-Intelligence Distinction*. New York: Holt, 1965.

Weber, Max. *Max Weber on Law and Sociology*. Cambridge: Harvard University Press, 1954.

White, E.B. Plimpton, George. ed. *The Paris Review Interviews, Eighth Series: Writers at Work*. New York: Penguin Books. 1988.

Whorf, Benjamin L. *Language, Thought, and Reality*. Cambridge: MIT Press, 1956

Wiesel, Elie. "Have you Learned the Most Important Lesson of All?" *Parade* 24 May 1992.

Winokur, Jon. *Advice to Writers*. New York: Pantheon, 1999.

Woolf, Virginia. "Moments of Being" in *A Sketch of the Past*. San Diego: Harcourt Brace Jovanovich, 1976.

The 9/11 Commission Report. Authorized Edition. New York: W. W. Norton & Company, 2004.

Quotation Bibliography

Abrahams, Lionel. *Journal of a New Man*. Johannesburg: Ad. Donker, 1984.

Adams, A.K. ed. *The Book of Humorous Quotations*. New York: Dodd Mead & Company, 1969.

Allen, Woody. "Spirit Departure." *Without Feathers*. London: Sphere Books, 1978.

Ehrlich, Barbara. *Renoir, His Life, Art and Letters*. New York: Harry N. Abrams, 1984.

Eigen, Lewis D., and Jonathan P. Siegel, Eds. *The Manager's Book of Quotations*. Rockville: Amacom, 1989.

Ellison, Harlan. *The Glass Teat*. Manchester: Savoy Books, 1978.

France, Anatole, tr. A. W. Evans. *Penguin Island*. New York: Heritage Press, 1947

Goldberg, Robert. *The Wall Street Journal* 13 Sept. 1993.

Hazlitt, William. *Quotationary.* New York: Random House, 2001.

Henderson, Bill. *Rotten Reviews.* New York: Penguin Books, 1987.

Hofstadter, Douglas, and Daniel C. Dennett. *The Mind's I: Fantasies and Reflections on Self and Soul.* London: Penguin Books, 1981.

Ionesco, Eugene. *Exit the King. The Manager's Book of Quotations.* Rockville: Amacon, 1989.

Jarrett, Derek. "Rogue Genius." In *The New York Review of Books* 22 Nov. 1990.

Juster, Norton. *The Phantom Tollbooth.* London: William Collins Sons, 1962.

Kung Fu Meditations & Chinese Proverbial Wisdom. Ed. Ellen Kei Hua. California: Farout Press, 1974.

Lewis, Alec. ed. *The Quotable Quotation Book.* New York: Thomas Y. Crowell, 1980.

Milne, Alan Alexander. "Tiggers Don't Climb Trees." In *The House at Pooh Corner.* New York: E.P. Dutton, 1956.

Pepper, Frank S. ed. *The Wit and Wisdom of the 20th Century.* New York: Peter Bedrick Books, 1987.

Poincare, Henri. "Mathematical Creation." *The Foundations of Science.* Science Press, 1946.

Quine, W.V. *Quiddities: An Intermittently Philosophical Dictionary.* London: Penguin Books, 1987.

Rating The Movies. Eds. Consumer Guide and Jay A. Brown. New York: Beekman House, 1986.

Richards, Dick. *The Wit of Peter Ustinov.* London: Leslie Frewin, 1969.

Rowes, Barbara, Ed. *The Book of Quotes.* New York: E.P. Dutton, 1979.

Sagar, Keith. *D. H. Lawrence.* London: Penguin Books, 1986.

Slonimsky, Nicolas. *Lexicon of Musical Invective.* Seattle: University of Washington Press, 1969.

Smith, Patricia. "Oriana Fallaci." *The Boston Globe,* 5 Jan 1993.

Solomon, Maynard. *Beethoven.* New York: Schirmer Books, 1977.

Spender, Stephen. "The Making of a Poem." In the *Partisan Review.* Summer 1946.

Theroux, Paul. "The Cerebral Snapshot." *Sunrise with Seamonsters, Travels and Discoveries 1964-1984*. London: Hamish Hamilton, 1985.

—. "Being a Man." *Sunrise with Seamonsters, Travels and Discoveries 1964-1984*. London: Hamish Hamilton, 1985.

Warren, Robert Penn, *American Arts* interview.

Watson, Derek. *Richard Wagner, A Biography*. New York: Schirmer Books, 1981.

Whitman, Walt. "Song of Myself." *Leaves of Grass* 1892 ed. New York: Bantam Books, 1983.

Winokur, John, Ed. *Writers on Writing*. Philadelphia: Running Press, 1986

Zilbergeld, Bernie, *The Shrinking of America, Myths of Psychological Change*. Boston: Little Brown & Co., 1983.

Index

Abominable Snowman, 113
Absolute/s, 69, 72, 73; and absolute truth, 69; and intolerant absolutes, 73
Acclaim, 83
Accommodate, 3, 111
The Act of Creation, 130
Actors, 129
Adaptability, 3, 40, 131-133; and adaptive skill, 112
Advertisers/Advertising, 24, 25, 32
Alienation, 79, 93
Allen, Woody, 71
Aloneness, 29-35, 93, 135
Alternatives, 23, 43, 95; and alternate lives, 109; and alternate self, 110
Ambiguous/Ambiguity, 11, 48, 95, 99, 134
American National Theater, 92
Amusing Ourselves To Death, 83
Ancient Egypt, 111
Ancient Greece, 27
Anderson, Hans Christian, 56
Answers, 40, 42, 98-99
Ante, xii
Anxiety, 22, 89, 127
Apartheid, 73
Arieti, Silvano, 11, 31, 75, 98-99
Arnold, Matthew, 59
Art, xii, 13, 44
Artists, 13
Asimov, Isaac, 10, 55, 93, 121, 130, 134
Atari, 132
Atom, 108,
Attention, 9, 22, 23, 56, 83, 84, 89, 97, 107, 108, 118, 127, 147; and inattention, 80
Atwood, Margaret, 32
Authenticity, 22, 83, 134, 136

Authority, 11, 22, 80, 108; and authoritarian, 138
Awareness, 147, 148
Banville, John, 73
Barbie, 32, 103
Barriers, 15
Bartok, 58
Baxter, Charles, 129
Beethoven, Ludwig van, 58
Being/non-being, 124
Being There, 82
Benzene, 108
Berlin, Isaiah, 74, 98
Bettelheim, Bruno, 25
Bible, 10
Bisociation, 130
Blinkered Thinking, 93-95
Bohr, Nels, 108
Bondage, 93
Book of Nurture, 126
Borge, Victor, 140
Boston Globe, 123
Boston Shakespeare Company, 90
Boundaries, 3, 93, 148
Bradbury, Ray, 96
Brazil, 92
Brazzi, Rossano, 48
British Royal Family, 54
British political scene, 70
Brown, Charlie, 125
Bushnell, Nolan, 132
Business, 113
Cantor, Eddie, 16
Carver, Raymond, 33
Categories, 46-47, 94, 138; and categorical apartheid, 46-48

Censorship, 42, 72, 92; and group censorship, 92; and self-censorship, 71, 93; and inner censor, 96; and uncensored, 99, 109
Chance, 82
Charlie Brown & Charlie Schulz, 40, 127
Child/Children, 24, 26, 39-42, 53, 54, 53, 56, 80-81, 84, 85, 92, 101, 111-114; 125-126 and childhood, 3, 27, 81, 111-114; and microwave child, 25; and programmed child, 25, 84; and childlike vision, 113, 114
Children's stories, 132
Children's book illustrations, 132, 133
Chinese cookery, 27
Choice, 21, 22, 23, 27, 98, 109, 141, 142, 147, 148; and no choice, 127
Chopin, Frederic, 58
Cleansing, 79; and ethnic cleansing, 79, idea cleansing, 79, religious cleansing, 79
Cleary, Beverly, 113
Cleese, John, 48, 70
Clinton, Bill, 124
Clinton, Hillary Rodham, 82
Cocteau, Jean, 24
Coercion, 69, 72
Coles, Robert, 92
Collaboration/ Collaborative Creativity, xii, 4, 108, 113, 133-139
Collectives, 81
Collusion, 120
Combine/Combinations, 10, 55, 148
Commercial, 26, 27, 81, 132; and commercial idea, 11, commercial potential, 32, commercial product, 12, 83
Commitment/Committed, 22, 27, 121-123, 135, 138, 141, 148
Committees, 137
Companion, xii
Completion, 26, 121, 122, 127, 128, 135
Compromise, 31, 120
Concept, 60, 118-121, 139; and concept sharing, 139, and concept conveyance 139, and conception, 60; and conceptualize; and preconception, 11
Confidence, 4, 57, 60, 91
Conformity, 15
Connectivity, 49, 109, 110, 130-131, 132, 148; and connections, 134, 140, emotional connections, over-reliance on connections, 85

Conscious/Consciousness, 10, 43, 57, 107, 109, 147; and conscious control, 11, conscious awareness, 99, 131, conscious mind; and self-conscious, 137
Consensus, 74, 81
Consumables, 25
Consumers/Consumerism, 21, 43
Control, 31, 40, 53, 69, 72, 73, 80, 95, 99, 136; and conscious control, 11, group control, 73, 82, negative control, 16; and controller, 43
Conventional, 140
Courage, xii, 3, 4, 82, 94, 95, 99
The Courage to Create, 94
Cousins, Norman, 15
Crawford, Joan, 54
Creativogenic, 33
Crichton, Michael, 48
Critic/Criticism, 40, 53, 56, 58-65, 90, 93, 137, 140, 147; and critical expectations, 112, critical voices, 90, 92, critical thinking, 41, 71
Culture, 44, 69, 72, 74, 81, 83; and cultural bouillabaisse, 74, cultural diversity, 74, cultural illusion, 81, cultural vitality, 74; and label culture, 46-48
The Culture of Narcissism, 83
Curricula (school), 40, 101
Czechoslovakia, 13, 34, 72
Dahl Gary, 32
Darrow, Charles, 123
Darwin, Charles, 10
Daydreams, 25
Deadlines, 127-128, 136, 138
De Bono, Edward, 97
Decisions, 22, 128; and indecision, 141; and decisiveness, 137
De Gaulle, Charles, 98
Destructivity, 79
Details, 21, 55, 130
Di Capua, Michael, 132
Diderot, Denis, 72
Dietrich, Marlene, 54
Differences, 74, 91
Dillard, Annie, 32
Dirty Dawg, 113
The Disappearance of Childhood, 40
Discipline, 23, 120, 122, 126, 135; and disciplines, 136
Disinformation, 21

Disney, Walt, 113
Divergent (thinking), 95
Diversity, 74
Dogmatism, 44, 72, 72, 97-98
Domain, 4
Doppelganger, 111
Drawing, 112
Drawing on the Right Side of the Brain, 112
Dreams (day and night dreams) 105-114; and dream deprivation, 105-114
Drill (and drill and kill) 39-42
Dubliners, 10
Duck, Donald, 113
Economic, 94
Education /Educated, 26, 39-42, 43, 94, 101, 122, 125, 126, 130, 133; and educative influences, 117
Edwards, Betty, 112
Ego, 108, 137
Egypt (Ancient), 111
Egypt, 73
Einstein, Albert, 12, 90
Elephants, 140
Email, 23, 24
Empathy, 128-129
Endurance, 148
Epiphany, 10
Eskimos, 44
Evaluation, 55-56
Even Cowgirls get the Blues, 114
Evolution, 10
Excuseologist, 47
Expectations, xi, 53-54, 82, 84, 110, 112, 127; and critical expectations, 112
Experience, 120, 122, 128, 129, 138, 142; and developmental experience, 111
Experts, 22
Facts, 40, 42
Failure, xii, 90-91, 97
Fairy Tales, 26, 27, 56, 82
Fallaci, Oriano, 123
Families, 23, 53, 54, 69, 71, 75, 83, 84, 120, 128; and familial influences, 117
Families and How to Survive Them, 70
Fanaticism, 73, and fanatical fervor, 97
Fantasy, 25, 111, 111, 112, 113, 114, 126
Farrar, Strauss & Giroux, 132
Fatwa, 73
Fear, 21, 59, 69, 73, 84, 87-103, 109, 118, 128, 137, 141; and fear of being different, 91-93; and fear of failure, 90-91; and fear of solitude, 33
Feelings, 14, 107
Fervor, 79
Feynman, Richard, 11
Film, xii
Flannelgraph, 47
Flashin', 124-125
Flexibility, 40, 100; and inflexibility, 76
Flight Patterns, 91
The Flintstones, 113
Fortune 500, 32
Fractionalization, 25
Frames of the Mind, 55
France, 98
Franklin, Benjamin, 16
Freedom, 148
French literature, 28
Frisbee, 32
Gardner, Howard, 55
Gates, William, 82, 141
Gender, 101
Gergen, Kenneth J., 23-24
Gestapo, 72
G.I. Joe and G. I. Joe nurses, 102
Gilbert and Sullivan, 92
Glimpse of possibility, xii
Goofy, 113
Gordimer, Nadine, 73
Gould, Stephen Jay, 130
Grass, Gunter, 113, 114
Greece (Ancient), 27
Grey, Zane, 48
Groups, 69, 70, 73, 80, 133, 134, 133-139; and group control, 71, 80, group cooperation, 3, group hate, 80, 133, group thinking, 69
Handler, Elliot & Ruth, 32
Hanna-Barbera, 113
Harmony, 137
Hasbro, 102
Hassenfeld Brothers, 102
Hate, 21, 41, 42, 69, 70, 73, 79, 80, 133
Havel, Vaclav, 12, 34, 46
Haven in a Heartless World, 45
Hierarchy of Motives, 14
Hoffman, Banesh, 10
Hofstadter, Douglas, 111
How-to, 4, 43, 44; and how-to-feel, 43; and how-to-feel ill, 44
Howe, Elias, 108
Huckleberry Hound, 113

Huggins, Henry, 113
Hula-Hoops, 32
Humor, 140-141
Huxley, Aldous, 107
Ideas, 5, 14, 25, 29, 31, 39, 40, 42, 44, 46, 49, 55, 57, 59, 69, 70, 72, 74, 82, 89, 93, 94, 95, 96, 97, 98, 102, 118, 119, 131, 134, 136, 137, 148; and budding ideas, 70, commercial ideas, 11, scientific ideas,11, spontaneous ideas, 126; and idea generation, 99; and structural ideal 119; and ideational fluency, 55
Ideologies, 42, 70; and ideological thinking, 46, 73, 98
Iglesias, Julio, 48
Illusion, 81, 82
Image/s, 11, 12, 35, 79, 82, 83, 94, 107, 109, 141; and visual image, 127; and image politics, 83
Imitation, xii, 80-81, 101, 120
Impulse, 80, 99, 121, 133
In the Night Kitchen, 132
Inattention, 78
Inauthenticity, 77-85
Indecision, 141-142; and indecisive people, 141-142
Individualism, 98
Indoctrination, 41
Industrial Revolution, 100
Inflexibility, 76
Information, 21, 22, 41, 43, 44, 48, 82, 97, 98, 107, 131
Ingredients, 22, 43, 91, 111, 140; and final ingredients 115-142; and active ingredients, 145
Inhibit/Inhibitors, 3, 4, 14, 137
Inner lives, 124; and inner motivations, 33, inner needs, 22
Innovation, 10, 74, 91
Internet, 23, 25, 79
iPods, 33
Inshallah, 123
Instincts, 12, 22, 43, 90, 107, 108, 129, 131, 140
Instruction, 37-40, 41, 42; and emotive instruction, 37-40; and instructional intrusion, 37, 39-42
Intelligence, 55, 56, 89, 119, 130, 131, 133; and Intelligent Tests (I.Q.); 55; and intellectual, 140
Intrusion, 112, 147; and emotional intrusion, 37; and instructional intrusion, 37; and judgmental intrusion, 51

Intuition/Intuitive, 4, 9, 10, 12, 13, 14, 22, 35, 81, 97, 127, 129, 130, 134; and non-intuition, 134
I.Q. tests, 55
Irving, John, 113
Jahanbegloo, Ramin, 98
The Jetsons, 113
Jitterbug Perfume, 114
Jordan, Michael, 82
Joy, xi, 90, 122, 124, 125-127, 134; and joyless, 125
Joyce, James, 9
Judgment, 58, 69, 70, 71, 90, 96, 109, 127, 128, 148; and judgmental intrusion, 51; and misjudged, 93; and unjudgmental, 147
Jung, Carl, 21, 94, 107
Ka, 111
Kafka, Franz, 72
Kekule, Friedrich, 108
Kiley, Brian, 44
Knowledge, 3, 10-11, 27, 41, 43, 74, 120, 122, 130, 136, 141; and accumulated knowledge, 107; and instant knowledge, 27
Koestler, Arthur, 130
Kosinski, Jerzy, 82
Labels/ Label-intensive, 45, 46, 47, 48
Landlord's Game, 123
Language, 42; and English language, 45
Lasch, Christopher, 45, 83
Lateral Thinking, 94, 95, 97
Legitimate power, 69
Li'l Folks, 125
Linn, Susan, 24
Linus, 47
Listen to the Mustn'ts, 96
Literature, xii, 59, 92, 94, 126, 132; and Literary criticism, 59
Liszt, Franz, 57
Local Anaesthesia, 113
Locke, John, 40
Loneliness, 89
Loopy De Loop, 113
Los Angeles Festival, 92
Lucy, 47
Lucky accident, xii
Lunch, 14-16
Lunch invitation, 14
MacArthur Foundation Fellowship, 55, 92, 130
Madonna, 82

Magimagician, 97
Mahfouz, Naguib, 73
Make-believe, 111
Making a Good Script Great, 137,
Maslow, Abraham, 15
Mason, Jackie, 45
Mattel, 24, 32, 103
Maugham, Somerset, 48
May, Rollo, 92, 125
Mcluhan, Marshall, 93
McNeal, James, 24
Mead, George Herbert, 75
Media, 24, 46, 82, 137
MGM, 113
The Mickey Mouse Club, 26
Microsoft, 82, 141
Middle Ages, 59
Mindlessness, 71, 79-80, 82, 101, 139
The Mind's Eye, 111
Mistakes, 90, 91, 141
Mob thinking, 71, 79
Mommie Dearest literature, 54
Monopoly, 122
Moss, Robert, 108
Mother Theresa, 82
Motivations, 16, 33, 80, 81, 84, 136, 137; and hierarchy of motives, 15
Mouse, Minnie, 113
Mouse, Ralph, 113
Mozart, Wolfgang, Amadeus, 92
Mtshali, Mbuyiseni Oswald, 73
Music, xii, 57-58, 94
My Friend, Albert Einstein, 11
My Speech to the Graduates, 71
Nabikov, Vladimir, 33
National Book Award, 11
Negativity, 95-97, 117, 147; and negative effects, 60; negative controls, 16
Networking, 85
New York Medical College, 11
New York Times, 16, 54
Nicaragua, 92
Nobel Prize, 11, 73, 108
Northern Canada, 92
Northern Ireland, 92
Norton, Juster, 97
Nutkin, Squirrel, 91
Online games, 25
Options, 21, 33
Optimism, xi, xii
Original/Originality, 4,15, 23, 26, 39, 42, 45, 80, 81, 118, 134, 137

Otherselves, 41, 80-81
Other/Otherism, 41, 70, 91, 133
Overload, 21
Palaeolithic artists, 74
Paradise Lost, 13
Paranoia, 70
Parents, 24, 54
Parker Brothers, 123
Passion, 23, 53, 84, 85, 117, 124-125, 146; and passionately richer, 121-122, 148
Passivity, 4, 26, 38, 40, 98, 118, 120
Paton, Alan, 72
Peanuts, 40, 47, 125, 127
Pensees Philosophiques, 72
Perception, 4, 23, 44, 74, 95
Perfect, 93; and past perfect, 93, 123
Perseverance, 119
Pet Rock, 32,
The Phantom Tollbooth, 96
Philosophy/Philosophical, 59, 69, 79, 82, 138
Piaget, Jean, 111
The Picture of Dorian Gray, 111
Pirsig, Robert, 127
Place, 31
Plunket, Robert, 54
Poland, 92
Politics, 12, 134; and political correctness, 133, political environment, 132, political influences, 117, political leaders, 83, political opportunists, 23, political situations; and British political scene, 70; and politicians, 81, 83
Pong, 132
Postman, Neil, 40, 42, 83
Potential, 4, 16, 56, 90, 109, 129, 147; and commercial potential, 32, creative potential, 14, 42, intellectual potential, 42, creative potential, 81; and potential interests, 85, potential selves, 129
Potter, Beatrice, 91
Power, 69, 73, 85, 137
Practice, 4
Prescription, 39
Product, 13, 26, 46, 56, 57, 118, aesthetic product, 12, commercial product, 12, creative product, 57, scientific product, 12; and production, 118, 119, 127, 134; and unproductive, 128
Program/Programming, 25, 26, 27; and programmed children, 27, programmed adults, 27; and twelve-step program, 45
Prokofiev, 57

Propoganda, xii, 12
Psychiatry/psychoanalysis, 94
Puddleduck, Jemima, 91
Pulitzer Prize, 92, 111
Purpose, 60, 108, 121-123
Quantum electrodynamics, 11
Queen Elizabeth, 56, 84
Question, 41, 42, 80, 81, 92, 98, 99, 147 and self-questioning, 122; and unquestioning, 81, 82, 101
Quimby, Ramona, 113
R's (the Three), 40
Rabbit, Peter, 91
Ravel, 58
Reagans, 54
Recovery, 45
Reed, Ishmael, 74
Religion, 45, 69, 73; and religious cleansing, 79, religious environment, 132
Repertoires, 93, 103
Repression, 22, 67- 76, 142
Restrictions, 3, 93
Resumed, 84-85
Rhodes, Hugh, 126
Right-brained, 9
Rigid, 93
Risk, 89, 90, 91, 93, 117, 140, 141, 148
Robbins, Tom, 35, 113, 114
Role-bound, 101-103; and role models 82-83
Rosten, Leo, 74
Routines, 93, 94, 128
Royal Family, 54
Ruddock, E.H., 102
Rules, 93, 100, 101; and rule-bound, 100-101
Rushdie, Salman, 57, 73
Russia, 73, 98
Sacrifice, 13, 28, 98, 110, 119, 122, 123-124
Sapir, Edward, 44
Sapir-Whorf Hypothesis, 44
The Satanic Verses, 57, 72
Satisfaction, 13,
Saturated, 27
The Saturated Self, 24
The Saturday Review, 16
Schroeder, 40
Schulz, Charles, 125, 127
Science/Scientific, 132, 135, 136, 137
Scrutiny, 51
Seger, Linda, 119, 137
Self-actualization, 4, 15, 90, 141, self-censorship, 71, self-congratulation, 138, self-conscious, 85, self-critical, 71,
self-definition, 138, self-direction, 4, self-help, 44,
selfhood,/sense-of-self, 60,
self-involvement, 45,
self-motivation, 4, self-pity, 123,
self-preservation, 123
Sellars, Peter, 92
Sendak, Maurice, 132
Severance from childhood, 111-114
Severance from night and daydreams, 107-110
Severance from Self, 110-111
Sewing machine, 108
Shakespeare, William, 92
Shekerjian, Denise, 92, 130
The Silencers, 72, 97
Silverstein, Shel, 96
Singer, Jerome, 109, 110, 111
Sketch of the Past, 124
Skinny Legs and All, 114
Skynner, Robin, 70, 80
Slaughter, Frank, 48
Smart Phones, 24
Smith, Patricia, 123
The Smurfs, 113
Snow White, 83
Social/Sociable, 34, 132; and social circumstances, 3; social commitments, 23, social consensus, 81, social environment, 3, 132, social influences, 117, social interaction, 34, social rewards, 125
Society, xii, 3, 42, 44, 69, 75, 76, 83, 91, creativogenic society, 75; label-intensive society, therapeutic society; and societal expectations, 101; and free society, 75
Solitude, 29, 31, 33, 34, 123; and solitary, 135; and fear of solitude, 33
Solutions, 22, 41, 93, 99; and solution-bound, 98-99; and adequate solutions, instant solutions, 98, 99, 142
Solzhenitsyn, Alexander, 73, 98
South Africa, 72, 92
South East Asia, 92
Sparky, 125
Specialization, 48, 49, 139; and overspecialization, 48
Speed Buggy, 113
Spiritual/Spirituality, 24
The Spiritual Life of Children, 92

Spofford, Otis, 113
Spontaneity/Spontaneous, 3, 11, 35, 84, 107, 126, 140
Standardized Tests, 55
Step-by-step thinking, 94
Stevenson, Robert Louis, 108, 111
Stimulation/stimulus, 9, 22, 25, 26, 33, 35, 42, 74, 84, 89, 90, 97, 98, 121, 127, 135, 138, 139, 149
Stock-taking, 117-118
The Strange Case of Dr. Jekyll and Mr. Hyde, 111
Strauss, Johann, 57
Stravinsky, Igor, 57, 58
Subconscious, 57
Swarthmore College, 22
Tabula rasa, 40
Tchaikovsky, Peter, Ilyitch, 57
Teamwork, 133-139,
Techniques, 122, 139
Technology, 41, 100, 136; and technologically-saturated, 23; and technological developments, 100
Television, 23, 24, 33, 79, 82, 83, 113, 114, 137
Tenacity, 120
Terror/terror attacks, 21, 79, 139; and intellectual terrorism, 72
Text Messaging, 25
Theology, 59
Therapeutic society, 45
Thinking/Thought, 33, 41, 48, 74, 79, 80, 82, 94, 96, 111, 129, 145; and blinkered thinking 93-95, boring thinking, 39, 117, convenient thinking, 85, corporate thinking, 100, creative thinking, 4, 15, 42, 80, 98, 139, critical thinking, 41, 71, deeper thinking, 98, divergent thinking, 95, diverse thinking, 73, educated thinking, 134, effective thinking, 139, experimental thinking, 98, explorative thinking, 41, group thinking, 69, homogeneous thinking, 81, 95, independent thinking, 44, 73, 80, 101, 133, ineffective thinking, 99, intelligent thinking, 4, 44, 73, 75, 82, 103, 135, lateral thinking, 94, 95, 97, linear thinking, 95, mindless thinking, 79, 139, mob thinking, 71, 74, 79, narcissistic-thinking, 45, non-thinking, 39, original thinking, 101, pigeon-hole thinking, 46, 48, responsible thinking, 71, standardized thinking, 148, step-by-step thinking, 94, versatile thinking, 133, vertical thinking, 94, 95; and thinking skills, 94; and thinkers-by-number, 37, 39; and thought processes, 82; and thoughtless, 23; and pre-thought, 9; and Thought Patrols, 67, 69, 70, 96
Thompson, Robert, 74
The Tin Drum, 113
Tom and Jerry, 113
Totalitarianism, 72
Towne, Robert, 129
Toy, Leland, 91
Truth, 40, 69, 79, 80, 98, 140
Turner Broadcasting, 113
Uncommon Genius, 92, 130
Unconscious, 10, 107, 109, 147
Unexpected ideas, xii
Vegimator, 47
Vertical thinking, 94, 95
Victim, 123
Victimization, 45
Visibility, 69, 83-84, 109,
Vitalogy, 101
Vocabulary, 44-46
Wagner, Richard, 57
Walker, Margaret, 33
Wallace, Alfred Russell, 10
Wallach, Michael, 55
Warner Communications, 132
Weber, Max, 69
Weston, Stanley, 102
Wham-O, 32
Where the Wild Things Are, 132
White, E.B., 33
Whorf, Benjamin Lee, 44
Wiesel, Elie, 73
Wilde, Oscar, 111
Wit, 140
Woolf, Virginia, 124
Xenophobia, 79
Yogi Bear, 113

Quotation Index

Abrahams, Lionel, 71
Albery, James, 128
Alcoholics Anonymous, 63
Allen, Woody, 111
American Art Journal, 64
Asimov, Isaac, 72
Babylonian Talmud, 82
Bacon, Francis, 48
Beethoven, Ludwig van, 64
Bell, Alexander, 136
Bellow, Saul, 112
Bennett, Arnold, 65
Bentley, Edmund Clerihew, 46
Berlin, Irving, 58
Bevan, Aneurin, 141
Billings, Josh, 51
Brezhnev, Leonid, 63
Burroughs, William, 108
Carlyle, Thomas, 62
Catherine A The Great@, 137
Cavett, Dick, 65
Chandler, Raymond, 124
Cheever, John, 130
Chinese Proverb, 90, 12
Churchill, Winston, 63
Clarke, James, 120
Clayton, Rawson, 63
Coward, Noel, 64
De San Concordio, Batholommeo, 94
Einstein, Albert, 55
Ellison, Harlan, 43
Emerson, Ralph Waldo, 91, 96
Evers, Medgar, 72
Fallaci, Oriana, 102
France, Anatole, vii
Freud, Anna, 54
Freud, Clement, 61
Gandhi, Mahatma, 19

George, David Lloyd, 63
Gershwin, George, 61
Gilbert, William Schwenck, 84
Gilman, Lawrence, 61
Godkin, E.L., 51
Goldberg, Robert, 25
Goldwyn, Samuel, 62
Hayakawa, S. I. 77
Hazlitt, W, 147
Holmes, Oliver Wendell, Jr., 100
Hubbard, Elbert, 65
Ionesco, Eugene, 19
Irving, Washington, 122
Jung, Carl Gustav, 87, 134
Juster, Norman, 75
Kael, Pauline, 65
Kirkus Review, 61
Koestler, Arthur, 89
Krishnamurti, Jiddu, 99
Kroneberger, Louis, 65
Kung Fu, 77
Lamb, Charles, 62
Lawrence, D.H. 105
Levinson, Daniel, 135
Lippman, Walter, 80
Mayo, Dr. William J., 49
Milne, A.A., 149
Moravia, Alberto, 115
Mortimer, Raymond, 62
Mozart, Wolfgang Amadeus, 32
Myhrvold, Nathan, 15
Nabokov, Vladimir, 61
Nietzche, George Wilhelm, 61, 86
Nin, Annais, 97
Ozick, Cynthia, 123
Peyser, H.F., 61
Picasso, Pablo, 62, 13, 132
Poincare, Henri, 10

Price, Luther D. 80
Quine, W.V., 42
Rating the Movies, 62
Rawson, Clayton, 65
Reagan, Ronald, 63
Renard, Jules, 119
Rusk Dean, 22
Sagan, Carl, 143
Sayers, Dorothy, 126
Schank, Robert C., 34
Skinner, B.F., 53
Spender Stephen, 7
Styron, William, 34
Thatcher, Margaret, 63
Theroux, Paul, 102
Toscanini, Arturo, 58, 64
Ustinov, Peter, 39, 65, 134
Van der Post, Laurence, 67
Wagner, Richard, 61
Warren Robert Penn, 29
Wells, H.G., 64
White, E.B., 64
Whitman, Walt, 37
Wiesel, Elie, 70, 139
Wilde, Oscar, 64
Yiddish proverb, 92
Zilbergeld, Bernie, 45